How to Rea

How to Read Your
ASTROLOGICAL
CHART

Aspects of the Cosmic Puzzle

DONNA CUNNINGHAM, MSW

WEISERBOOKS
Boston, MA / York Beach, ME

First published in 1999 by
Red Wheel/Weiser, LLC
P. O. Box 612
York Beach, ME 03910-0612

Library of Congress Cataloging-in-Publication Data

Cunningham, Donna.
How to read your astrological chart : aspects of the cosmic puzzle /
Donna Cunningham.
p. cm.
Includes bibliographical references and index.
ISBN 1-57863-114-9 (pbk : alk. paper)
1. Horoscopes. I. Title.
BF1728.A2C86   1999
133.5′4—dc21   99-37880
                                                CIP

EB
Typeset in 11 point Adobe Caslon
Cover and text design by Kathryn Sky-Peck

Computer generated charts by Astrolabe, Brewster, MA, using Solar Fire

PRINTED IN THE UNITED STATES OF AMERICA

08 07 06 05 04 03 02 01
10 9 8 7 6 5 4 3 2

The paper used in this publication meets the minimum requirements of the
American National Standard for Information Sciences—Permanence of Paper for
Printed Library Materials Z39.48-1992(R1997).

~

This book is dedicated to the beloved friends and supporters who make my phone bill a living nightmare each and every month—Gretchen Lawlor, Gail Branson, Joyce Liechenstein, Nicoli Bailey, Bill Baeckler, and my sister/webmaster, Dian Hill.

Table of Contents

List of Charts ... xi

List of Tables ... xi

Acknowledgments ... xii

Introduction ... xiii

CHAPTER ONE

Looking a Chart in the Face ... 1

First, check the birth time; a visual survey of the chart; planets on the angles; the house-cusp controversy revisited—again; full house, empty house; finding aspects; another visual aid—drawing in aspects; looking for clusters; spotting themes in a chart; concluding the visual overview.

CHAPTER TWO

The Sun, Moon, and Ascendant—
Working Partners or Family Feud? ... 23

Separating out the functions of the Sun; the Ascendant and our family role; Sun versus Ascendant; how well do the Sun and the Ascendant work together?; a Sun-Ascendant clash—the comedienne Roseanne; bringing the Moon into the picture; how the

Moon and Ascendant relate to one another; pairing the Sun and Moon; combining Sun, Moon, and Ascendant; a trio in harmony—Candice Bergen; how aspects change the big three; clarifying these differences through transits; transits to the Sun—redefining the core self; Moon transits—crossing lunar thresholds.

CHAPTER THREE

Plugging in the Individual Planets . . . 47

Step one—dismantling the sign; how planets are affected by their signs; from keywords to descriptions; going deeper—making a list of planetary functions; integrating function and sign; the high road or the low road?; planets in houses; putting these techniques to work.

CHAPTER FOUR

What Planet Are You From? . . . 65

How planets become keynotes; the maid from Mercury—Goldie Hawn; what the planetary types are like; how signs and houses modify keynote planets; a denizen of Neptune and Pluto—Fabio; what can you do if you're not from this planet?

CHAPTER FIVE

A Guided Tour of the Hard Aspects . . . 81

Step one: making a concept list; step two: developing a psychological profile; the conjunction—shared viewpoints; an enhanced concept list; squares—conflict and miscommunication; the opposition—complementary element, conflicting mode; teeter-totter or tug-of-war?; opposite signs, opposite houses; putting the method to the test.

CHAPTER SIX

Soft Aspects—When the Living is Easy . . . 103

Trines—shared elements are the key; getting back on the Mercury-Saturn train; the sextile—an aspect of ease; a last look at Mercury and Saturn; Kurt Browning's sexy sextiles; the plot thickens—Kurt's opposition and squares; how would you like a soft life?

CHAPTER SEVEN

Piecing Together the Major Configurations . . . 119

Grand trines—too much of a good thing?; a born spiritual leader—the Dalai Lama; Willie Nelson and the finger of fate; sensitive down-home guy or cold-hearted cad?; Maya Angelou—the caged bird sings; looking for clusters; concluding the natal chart survey and moving on to transits.

CHAPTER EIGHT

Understanding Transits— Another Way to Use Aspects . . . 137

Which transits are important?; how long does a transit last?; developing concept lists for outer-planet transits; no place to hide—the transiting conjunction; squaring off for a fight—the transiting square; transiting oppositions and the other; transiting trines—reaping the harvest; transiting sextiles—lucky contacts; the transiting inconjunct—you've got to *feel* it; Rosie O'Donnell's success story—luck of the Irish, or just plain hard work?; and much, much more.

C H A P T E R   N I N E

An Overview of Transits—
Seeing the Whole Picture . . . 159

How important is a particular transit?; spotting critical zones and eras; "The sky is falling!"; an introvert's view of transits; "it's more complicated than that"; one man's Pluto is another man's poison; "How am I doing?"; facing the difficult potentials of a transit; "I'm allergic to Neptune!"; life-transforming transits to the four angles; the Millennial Challenge—getting past the personal to the universal.

C H A P T E R   T E N

How Aspect Analysis
Illuminates Chart Comparison . . . 185

Preparing for a relationship reading; the house configuration of each chart; conjunctions—the juice in chart comparison; the house placement of a conjunction; other aspects in chart comparison; and now you are on your own!

Bibliography . . . 195

Index . . . 197

About the Author . . . 204

List of Charts

Chart 1. Jeane Dixon 6
Chart 2. Jeane Dixon, a second version with three wheels . . . 7
Chart 3. Jeane Dixon, natal chart with aspects drawn in . . . 19
Chart 4. Roseanne 30
Chart 5. Candice Bergen. 39
Chart 6. Goldie Hawn 71
Chart 7. Fabio 78
Chart 8. Albert Einstein 87
Chart 9. Kurt Browning 111
Chart 10. The Dalai Lama XIV 122
Chart 11. Willie Nelson 127
Chart 12. Maya Angelou. 131
Chart 13. Rosie O'Donnell 157

List of Tables

Table 1. A Quick Guide to Finding Aspects. 15
Table 2. Mercury and Aquarius Blended. 52
Table 3. Positive and Negative Expressions of Mars
          in Pisces and Gemini 59
Table 4. Positive and Negative Expressions of Venus
          in Pisces and Gemini 60
Table 5. Venus in Pisces in the 6th or 9th House 62
Table 6. E.T. Cheat Sheet: What Planet Are
          You From? 68
Table 7. Processes You May Experience During an
          Outer-Planet Transit. 141
Table 8. A Transit-Tracking Table for 1980–2010 163

Acknowledgments

To *The Mountain Astrologer* for encouraging and publishing the column that was the kernel of this book and for permission to reprint the articles. To Gary Lorentzen, a seasoned astrologer and educator whose knowledge and guidance about curriculum design vastly improved the method taught in this book.

Introduction

How long have you been studying astrology? If you've been at it for a year and you still lack the confidence to tackle a horoscope, then the fault lies, not with your intelligence, but with the learning method you are using. No doubt you've been learning by rote—trying to memorize what your teacher, your books, and visiting lecturers have to say. These are all valuable sources of knowledge. You should benefit from all of them, as well as from the knowledge of other astrologers. Our field is richly blessed with gifted teachers, speakers, and authors, each with unique perspectives, experiences, and observations to offer. By all means, read their books and go to their lectures. My publishers and I certainly hope you read mine!

Rote learning, however, is flawed. It doesn't teach you to think for yourself or empower you to reason astrologically. All it prepares you to do is tap into bits of someone else's experience lodged in your brain. If your memory is Swiss cheese or if you haven't bought a book on a particular topic yet, you may draw a blank when handed a chart.

If astrology is no more than a memory trick, then you're only as good as your memory. You may be in trouble when confronted with something new—as we are, daily, in astrology because of the infinite number of planetary combinations and the ever-changing wheel of the zodiac. None of us were in our current bodies the last time Pluto was in Sagittarius, and a scant handful of us experienced the last transit of Uranus through Aquarius. No book or article can fully prepare us for new conditions like these. We're all flying by the seats of our pants, struggling to understand what these placements mean and how they operate.

Moreover, the exact combination of planets, houses, and signs in each chart is unique. Even if you read in several "cookbooks" what it means to have Mars and Uranus conjunct, how can you know what it's like when they're conjunct in Cancer in the 12th house? How would it be different for them to be conjunct in Virgo in the 2nd? What if they are conjunct in Virgo, but Saturn opposes them from Pisces? What will happen now that Pluto in Sagittarius is starting to square both ends of that opposition? You need to be able to reason astrologically to think through the different planetary combinations you continually encounter.

This is not a cookbook, so much as an anti-cookbook. This book is intended to free you from dependence on astrological cookbooks and give you the confidence—and the capacity—to read charts. Cookbook interpretations aren't bad. Lord knows, I've written plenty of them myself, and they're all valuable, up to a point. They become a liability, however, when you begin to believe that you can't read a chart yourself, but are stuck memorizing what Rob Hand or Noel Tyl or Donna Cunningham have to say.

You won't find all twelve of anything in this book. This is not a book in which you can look up all the aspects to your Venus and learn how to find your soul mate through astrology. Instead, this book teaches you to figure out for yourself the meaning of those Venus aspects, or your fixed T-square, or that upcoming Uranus transit to your Sun. Rather than encouraging you to learn by rote, it encourages you to reason astrologically. Step by step, you'll discover a structured approach. You'll combine various features, weighing and balancing them to see what is important.

That's a tall order, isn't it? In order for this book to succeed at its purpose, you'll have to work every bit as hard at absorbing and claiming the method for your own as I did in grappling with the material to get it across with precision. I often felt, in writing this book, that I was writing with an X-Acto knife rather than a word processor!

It will all be worth it, however, if it makes astrology flow through your veins like a living thing, rather than something you can only acquire second-hand. Don't you wish you could pick up a horoscope and begin to interpret it, rather than drag out your texts? If you want that, if your commitment to mastering astrology is that strong, then you're already on your way!

Many of you may think you can't do this. That insecurity is a legacy of rote learning. Trust me, you *can* do this. We'll do it together, here, step by step. With each successive chapter, you will put together a new piece of the cosmic puzzle.

If you're confused by a chart, it's probably too cluttered. If you've included seven or eight asteroids, a veritable sky-show of fixed stars, two kinds of progressions, and several dozen midpoints, no wonder you're overwhelmed. I'm not saying these techniques don't work. The trouble is that they all do. That's why it's tempting to include them all. To begin interpreting with ease, you must get the basics down before adding extras.

It's like living in a house that's too cluttered. You like everything you see, so you buy it. You go to the mall, you pick up some items. You go to a garage sale and pick up some more. Pretty soon, you can't even walk around because of the clutter and you're embarrassed to have anyone over. That kind of house is much harder to clean. It becomes such an overwhelming task that you just let it slide.

Astrology is much the same. Many of you have texts stacked to the ceiling. You've been to 88 workshops and have picked up so much information that you don't know where to begin. You probably feel cheated if you come away from a conference without a suitcase full of books and a notebook full of new rules and techniques. You've had the mental equivalent of a three-day binge—you're suffering from that same bloated feeling—but you congratulate yourself that now you *know* more. The trouble is that, when you get home and sit down to do a chart, you're even more overwhelmed. Now you have to figure out what to do with the Anti-vertex, Hades, Pholus, and hundreds of midpoints!

By contrast, you'll find that my style is minimalist—the standard natal chart and transits with few frills—and I recommend that you at least start out that way. This book talks about what works for me, but what works for you may be slightly different. It's up to you to decide which factors to include. You may get a wealth of information from Sabian symbols or the fifth harmonic. If so, include them. Just stay sparse and uncluttered so the cosmos' main messages stand out.

Lately, a movement called Voluntary Simplicity has been developing as an antidote to our harried, overcomplicated, modern lifestyle. It entails cutting back on addictive spending and compulsive accumulation of possessions to regain peace of mind. Surprisingly, the movement isn't coming from disciples of the latest Eastern guru, but from burnt out, chronically fatigued and frustrated, former denizens of the corporate rat race.

Advocates of Voluntary Simplicity are talking about creative downscaling, cutting up their credit cards, and moving back into smaller houses to get out from under crushing mortgage payments. They're throwing out masses of expensive, dust-gathering gadgets that mass marketing convinced them they needed, and they're resisting the thrall of new ones. Minds boggled by stimulus overload, they're unplugging the TV and canceling half their subscriptions. They're discovering that less is much, much more.

While many of us in astrology pride ourselves on being nonmaterialistic, this creative downscaling may hold some answers for us as well. Astrology, ruled by Uranus, is faddish and more responsive to cultural undercurrents than we like to acknowledge. During the inflationary '80s, when Uranus and Neptune were in expansive Sagittarius, we bit off more than we could chew. We added features in a wildly eclectic, scatter-gun fashion, with little structure and little thought about what to do with them once we had them.

As a result, when you work with my method, your first step forward may be two steps back. That is, to be more comfortable reading charts, you may have to retrench and get more basic. Just for now, go for bare-bones decor. Adopt the futon-on-the-floor style of astrology. Toss out the last five planetoids or significant points you stuck in, and breathe a sigh of relief. See if interpretation doesn't suddenly become easier.

—Donna Cunningham

How to Read Your Astrological Chart

CHAPTER ONE

Looking a Chart in the Face

After studying astrology for a while—ten months for some, ten years for others—you decide it's time to stop reading books and start reading charts. You pick one up and wonder how to proceed. You recall dozens of rules and techniques, some of which contradict each other. You stare at the chart. Confronted by a dizzying array of symbols, you try to figure out what's important. Over time, astrological sophisticates develop their own systems for reading horoscopes. This chapter, and the rest of this book, presents mine. This is not the only method for reading charts. You may not choose to use it. But this is the way I analyze charts in my practice. It identifies the most significant features in very short order.

First, Check the Birth Time

Begin by speculating on the accuracy of the data. Times that have been rounded off, like 7:00 or 7:30, are suspect. Times on the quarter-hour are likely to be closer to the truth, and a time like 7:06 may be exact. Be especially cautious when the Ascendant is in the last few degrees of one sign or the first few degrees of the next, since a slight difference in birth time can change the rising sign. In borderline cases, ask for the Sun sign of both parents, as one of them may be the correct Ascendant.

Ask where the person got the data. If it's from Mom's memory, she's 80, and she had seven kids, the data may be faulty unless memorable circumstances accompanied the birth. A birth announcement or baby book may be given some credence. If the time was noted on the birth certificate, it is at least as close as the delivery-room staff could make it.

However, when difficult planets like Saturn, Pluto, or Neptune fall near the Ascendant, inquire if any unusual circumstances accompanied the delivery. Often, there is quite a saga. If this was a chaotic (Neptune) or a particularly difficult birth (Saturn or Pluto), the data could well be in question. Especially in life-threatening circumstances, delivery-room staff pay attention to the baby and the mother, not the clock on the wall. Typically, when both stabilize and cleanup begins, someone will ask when the baby was born. The person in charge looks at the clock and makes a guess, and that guess is recorded for posterity.

Take the birthplace and year into account as well. Until 1967, observance of Daylight Savings Time was notoriously changeable from town to town and even year to year, especially in the Midwest. The best reference, at this writing, for checking this is *The American Atlas*, but even that is amended as new information comes to light.[1]

---

[1]Meticulously compiled by Mark Pottenger, Thomas Shanks, and Neil Michelsen, *The American Atlas* is an indispensible reference work for both time changes, and latitudes and longitudes (San Diego, CA: AstroComputing Services, 2nd edition, 1981).

In some areas—and some eras—state law has mandated that Standard Time be recorded on the certificate, rather than Daylight Savings Time. Illinois was such a state until 1959, as was Pennsylvania between 1921 and 1970. Where this rule was in effect, the birth certificate of someone born on May 25th at 9:00 P.M. EDT would read 8:00 P.M. Not all hospitals paid attention to the law—and not all delivery-room staff remembered it all the time. As a result, even the time on a birth certificate may not be recorded correctly.

For Pennsylvania and Illinois natives, you should definitely ask for the source of the time. A baby book or birth announcement notation may be based on clock time, and thus might be Daylight Savings Time. A parent's memory of the birth time may be from the clock (and thus Daylight Savings Time) or may be from a later glance at the birth certificate (and thus possibly Standard Time). For DST births, ask for a few key past events to double-check the Midheaven through transits or progressions. Despite precautions, errors may creep in, but at least you'll be forewarned.

That's bad enough, given that there are 186 timetables for Pennsylvania alone in *The American Atlas*. At least, for six months of the year, we don't have to worry about Daylight Savings Time—except for those born during World Wars I and II and the oil crisis of 1974-5, that is. However, just when I thought it was safe to fire up the software, I discovered that, if Pennsylvanians find a town name they like, they tend to use it more than once.

I surveyed one two-page spread—two of 26 pages of towns in Pennsylvania. Among the many redundancies were two Bethlehems, two Bryn Mawrs, three Bloomingdales, five Brooksides, and *seven* Bridgeports. (There may also be North and East Bridgeport and Old Bridgeport—they wouldn't be

listed on that page.) You also have to watch for spelling varia-
tions—there were two Bridgetons and one Bridgetown.

These towns are often far enough apart to produce several
degrees difference in Ascendants and Midheavens. Between the
two Bethlehems, there are three degrees difference on the
Midheaven and four on the Ascendant. That is enough to
throw predictions off seriously or change a rising sign. To avoid
error, ask the county of birth or the name of the nearest good-
sized city. (Pennsylvania isn't the only problem area—there are
three Brooklyns in New York state. Two are in the boonies a
considerable distance from New York City, but the one where
so many bright, funny, famous, and infamous folks were born is
73W56; 40N38.)

A Visual Survey of the Chart

Astrology is primarily a visual medium. Out of the five or six
usual senses, we each have one or two that we prefer. Some of
us are visually inclined, some are tactile, and some learn best by
hearing. If you're not particularly visual, you can train yourself
to see more acutely. You could accentuate color in drawing up a
wheel, as some astrologers do. They may use red ink for planets
in fire signs, green for earth, blue for water, and perhaps orange
for air. Another visual aid is the European system of drawing
houses their exact size rather than the illusory equal size (the pie
chart) of most printed charts.

Whatever devices you adopt, keep the wheel uncluttered.
As discussed in the introduction, I focus on the basic, no-frills
chart—the ten original planets[2] and outer-planet transits. In

---

[2]We'll call them ten planets to make it easy. There are eight planets and the Sun and
Moon, called luminaries in older textbooks.

actual practice, I start with a one-ring chart with just the natal placements. After analyzing them and drawing in the aspects by hand, I use a bright color to plot in house positions of the transiting outer planets and Jupiter. When a transiting planet shifts houses within the year, I draw a double-headed arrow showing before and after house positions.

One advantage of eliminating clutter is that important features stand out more starkly. Charts 1 and 2 give two renditions of the horoscope of astrologer/seeress Jeane Dixon to illustrate this. Chart 1 confines itself to bare bones (see page 6). The inner ring is her natal wheel and the ten traditional planets. The outer ring shows outer-planet transits at the time of her death on January 26, 1997. Chart 2 displays five asteroids, with transits in ring two, and solar-arc progressions in ring three (see page 7). Do you tense up just looking at the three-ringed version? If so, work with chart 1 until you are fluent enough not to get thrown by detail. Without getting into the meaning of anything on the page, determine what stands out visually. Which houses or sectors are emphasized, and which are empty? Where do planets clump together? Are there planets that leap out at you in any way—for instance, by being alone on one side of the chart while everything else is on the other side? Make a note of your observations, for these "standout" factors are likely to be important.

Start by ignoring the outer ring. Survey the inner ring and note that the planets are widely scattered, with only two empty houses. This is somewhat unusual—many people have four or five empty houses. Jot this down, as we'll look at houses later. You may also remark that several planets cluster near the Midheaven—not surprising for someone in the public eye. Let's explore what these observations mean.

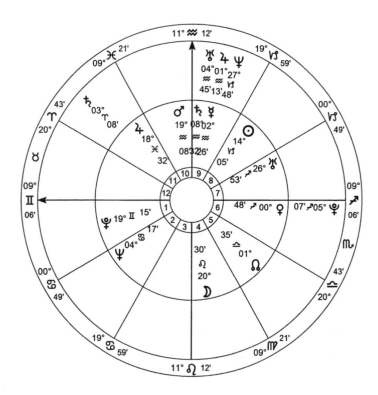

Chart 1. Jeane Dixon. According to her birth certificate, she was born January 5, 1904, at 2:00 P.M. CST +6:00, in Medford, WI, 45N09, 090W20. The information was printed in Lois Rodden's Data News #64, April, 1997. The chart is in the tropical zodiac, with Placidus houses. The inner ring is her natal chart; the outer ring shows outer-planet transits on the day of her death, January 26, 1997.

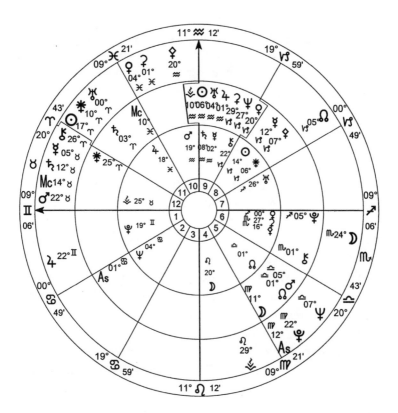

Chart 2. A second version of Jeane Dixon's chart with three wheels: the inner wheel is her natal chart, with five asteroids; the middle wheel shows the transiting outer planets and asteroids on the date of her death; and the outer wheel shows progressions on the date of her death.

Planets on the Angles

Use a broad-tipped marker to highlight planets up to 10 degrees on either side of the four angles—the Ascendant, Midheaven, Descendent, or IC (4th-house cusp). This includes planets in the 3rd, 6th, 9th, or 12th houses, as long as they are within 10 degrees of an angle. These crucial areas are the Gauquelin sectors, named for Françoise and Michel Gauquelin, the French psychologists who discovered them.

The Gauquelins made an invaluable contribution to our field by researching over 60,000 timed birth charts. In their meticulously designed studies, they consistently found that planets in those sectors affect public perception of the individual, to the extent that they are signatures. Their statistics showed that the strongest of the four regions are: within ten degrees of the Midheaven, but in the 9th house; and within 10 degrees of the Ascendant, but in the 12th house. The closer the planet is to the angle, the stronger its effect. The system, of course, depends on an accurate birth time.

We can only touch on their work, but you should read about it for a more complete picture—or to sway that skeptic in your life. I have used this method for over 25 years and find the highlighted planets consistently emphasized in client's lives. For instance, if Venus is highlighted, the person tends to be noticeably Venusian (e.g., concerned with relationships, appearances, and keeping the peace).

In Jeane Dixon's inner wheel, you will find six planets highlighted, an unusual number that probably increased her public visibility. Three of these are within 10 degrees of the Midheaven—Mercury and Saturn in the 9th house, and Mars in the 10th. Pluto is in the 1st house, 10 degrees from her Ascendant, Venus is in the 6th house, 9 degrees from the Descendant, and the Moon is in the 4th house, 9 degrees from the IC. Chapter four discusses the significance of each angular planet.

Another proof of the importance of angular placements is their effect in relocation charts and Astro*Carto*Graphy® maps. Part of the impact of a major geographic move is due to the shifting of new planets onto angles. That's why some folks thrive on Phoenix and hate Boston, or vice versa. Or why a recluse born with Pluto on the Ascendant can, at least partially, emerge from her cocoon by moving 3000 miles from her birth-place. The accuracy of this technique depends on a precise birth time, but the shifting of planets to new angles has the same result as moving Gauquelin sectors. Planets on relocated angles operate as keynotes in that region.

Situations that arise in various locations can even be used to double check the birth time's accuracy. Despite his respect for astrology—or possibly because of it—U.S. President Ronald Reagan's birth time has remained a mystery. Astrologers have enthusiastically espoused as many as twelve different Ascendants. Jim Lewis, who created Astro*Carto*Graphy®, put forth an interesting argument for Pisces. He pointed out that with Pisces Rising natally, Reagan's relocation to Washington, DC, put Mars in Capricorn near the Midheaven, the career and status angle. Capricorn is the sign of executives. Mars represents leadership, but is also connected with war, weapons (recall the Stealth Bomber), and, especially, guns (remember his near-assassination in Washington and the gun-control bill.)[3]

[3]Jim Lewis's rectification gives Reagan's data as February 6, 1911, at 8:25 A.M. CST, in Tampico, IL. The map appears in the *Astro*Carto*Graphy Book of Maps*, by Jim Lewis and Ariel Guttman (St. Paul, MN: Llewellyn Publications, 1989), p. 163.

The House-Cusp Controversy Revisited—Again

For at least twenty years, astrologers have disagreed about house divisions, often vociferously. The more scientifically-minded tend to espouse the Koch system, while diehards like myself stick with the traditional Placidus system. The knotty problem lies with the intermediate cusps, which may be in different signs in one or the other system. Moreover, some planets may change houses, depending on which system you use. Many people pick the system that puts their own planets in the best light. If their Venus falls in the self-defeating 12th in one system and the friendly 11th in another, they'll swear by the one that puts Venus in the 11th.

No one seems to disagree about the cusps of the 1st, 4th, 7th, and 10th houses. They are clearly demarcated and identical in all but the equal house system, which buries the true Midheaven and IC. They correspond with the four angles that showed up so sharply in the Gauquelin studies. A planet sitting on one of them carries extra power. They also correspond to four major reference points in space—the two horizons, the Zenith, and the Nadir. Unlike other house cusps, they are given their own names—the Ascendant, IC, Descendant, and Midheaven. These four points in space are nearly as active as a planet. If the birth time is exact, when a transiting or progressed planet forms an aspect to one of them, an event will usually occur. A progressed angle making an aspect to a natal position may also coincide with an event.

For all the above reasons, these four cusps are *real*. I am not entirely convinced of the reality of the remaining cusps. There is no such clear demarcation of the intermediate house cusps—2nd, 3rd, 5th, 6th, 8th, 9th, 11th, and 12th. Their degree, and even their sign, may vary with the house system. A planet that sits on one of these cusps does not gain in power. Events only occasionally occur when a planet crosses them by transit or progression. When they do, there is usually a natal planet in that numerical range that accounts for it (e.g., the house cusp is at 8 Libra, but there are planets at 8 Cancer and 8 Leo). Unlike the progressed angles, when a progressed intermediate house cusp forms an angle to a natal planet, it may not correspond to events.

If the intermediate cusps were real divisions rather than artificial ones, there wouldn't be such controversy about them. The truth would be self-evident. Instead of crisp dividing lines, there may be gray areas shading gradually from one house into another. I hold as suspect any planet within 5 degrees of an intermediate cusp.

I then question the person to determine which house seems to be the focus of that planet's energy. What these interviews clarify, more often than not, is that the planet on the cusp affects, and is affected by, the matters of both houses. Moreover, it appears to draw the two together. For instance, Venus on the 11th-12th cusp often shows up as a tendency to have secret, unrequited crushes on friends or even—until the person learns better—to engage in unhappy, illicit affairs within their circle of friends.

Full House, Empty House

When you scan a chart, some houses may appear empty, while others are relatively full. Here, I pay attention only to the basic ten planets, not to nodes, asteroids, or parts, because those basic planets represent major focuses and expenditures of energy. Given twelve houses and only ten planets, at least two houses will be vacant. However, when several planets clump together in a single house—as often happens with the Sun, Mercury, and Venus—even more houses will be unoccupied.

This is as it should be. We can only scatter our energies in so many directions before we become as fragmented as the asteroid belt. The person whose planets are deployed in many different houses tends to have many interests and to try to juggle many responsibilities and connections. Whether they are successful at it, or whether they become ineffectual dilettantes, depends on other factors in the chart. We can't know that from just looking at the house pattern. Jeane Dixon's natal planets are dispersed into nine different houses, and yet she did accomplish many things.

Full houses depict highly significant areas of life, not unlike putting lots of eggs in a single basket. The area in which we expend our energy is where we tend to get results. A full house is therefore, an area in which meaningful people, situations, and events are clustered. If you have several good planets in the 11th house, but nothing in the 4th, friends will be major supports and may outweigh family in importance in adulthood. Likewise, club officers often have significant 11th-house placements.

The matters governed by a house with a stellium, or containing the Sun and one or two other planets, can even be a career indicator. For instance, a friend with a stellium in the 3rd house started a very successful answering service. A travel agent had several planets in the 9th house. Many academics or spiritual teachers also have a 9th-house emphasis. The 8th house, when strong, can show mediumistic tendencies, and may also be an indicator of the potential for wealth. Jeane Dixon's Sun is in the 8th house.

Empty houses or sectors indicate that major planetary energy isn't being deployed toward matters of that house, but instead is focused elsewhere. Therefore, matters of that house are apt to take a back seat to matters of houses where planets are massed. A woman with no planets in the 4th or 5th house, but with the Moon in the 10th, is likely to be more fulfilled as a career woman than as a traditional homemaker.

Just don't conclude that an empty house means nothing will ever happen in the areas of life that house governs. One of Jeane Dixon's empty houses is the 3rd, signifying communication, and yet her columns and books have been the foundation of her success. In this case, Mercury and Gemini, both related to the 3rd house, more than compensate for the empty house, because she has Gemini rising and Mercury conjunct the Midheaven.

Many novices become upset if their 7th house is vacant, thinking it means they will never marry. Consider, however, what else in the chart may compensate. How strong is Venus? Are there major placements in Libra, especially the Sun, Moon, or Ascendant? Librans tend to marry, whether their choices are sound or not. Where is the ruler of the 7th house? If the ruler of the 7th is in the 4th, and the 4th is strongly tenanted, then forming a family and maintaining a homelife is a stronger drive than marriage itself. The marriage may be a means to that end.

Moreover, houses that are empty at birth don't remain empty throughout life. Transiting or progressed planets that move into an empty house tend to remain there for years. They stimulate new events and conditions in the matters of that house. A long transit of an outer planet through the 2nd house corresponds to a long series of developments in the individual's finances. If there are no planets in the 2nd house natally, that transit means the individual will devote an unaccustomed amount of attention to earning and managing money.

Remember what was said earlier about intermediate house cusps being gray areas rather than clear demarcations. You will often see a meaningful development when a transiting or progressed planet crosses an angle. However, don't expect instant action when one crosses an intermediate house cusp. Generally, though new conditions are shaping up, no action will take place until an aspect is formed to a natal planet or angle.

Finding Aspects

Another important preliminary is finding aspects—angular relationships of one kind or another between planets. How fluent are you at finding and interpreting aspects? If you aren't comfortable, focusing on them for several weeks or taking a class can pay off handsomely. Aspects are a key, not only to the birth chart, but to transits, progressions, and chart comparison. We will spend several chapters on this topic.

Counting houses to find aspects can be misleading. Except in the equal-house system, houses may vary in size, involve more than one sign, and contain interceptions, in which a pair of signs is missing from the cusps. A more sound approach is to count signs. An even better one is to memorize the relationships between signs, as shown in table 1 (page 15). We'll get more insight into this table in the chapters that follow. The more you understand about why signs are in harmony—or disharmony— the more fluent you become at analyzing aspects.

Work in a systematic fashion, so that you don't miss any aspects. Begin with the earliest planet in the zodiac, and draw in all its aspects. Then proceed to the next planet and the next, until you have done them all. In Jeane Dixon's natal chart (see chart 3, page 19), the earliest planet is Pluto in Gemini, followed by Neptune in Cancer and the Moon in Leo. The advantage to this method is that it is "astro-logical" and built on the sign relationships spelled out in Table 1.

With a computer chart, the grid at the side locates aspects. However, don't rely on the computer to do all the work of finding them. What if there's a power outage and you're trying to discover why the power went out? Suppose someone at an astrol-

Table 1: A Quick Guide to Finding Aspects.

TYPE OF ASPECT		Sextile	Square	Trine	Quincunx	Opposite
DISTANCE APART		2 signs	3 signs	4 signs	5 signs	6 signs
SUGGESTED ORBS		2-4°	5-6°	5-6°	2-3°	8°
SIGN TYPE	**SIGN**					
Cardinal Fire	♈	♊, ♒	♋, ♑	♌, ♐	♍, ♏	♎
Fixed Earth	♉	♋, ♓	♌, ♒	♍, ♑	♎, ♐	♏
Mutable Air	♊	♌, ♈	♍, ♓	♎, ♒	♏, ♑	♐
Cardinal Water	♋	♍, ♉	♎, ♈	♏, ♓	♐, ♒	♑
Fixed Fire	♌	♎, ♊	♏, ♉	♐, ♈	♑, ♓	♒
Mutable Earth	♍	♏, ♋	♐, ♊	♑, ♉	♒, ♈	♓
Cardinal Air	♎	♐, ♌	♑, ♋	♒, ♊	♓, ♉	♈
Fixed Water	♏	♑, ♍	♒, ♌	♓, ♋	♈, ♊	♉
Mutable Fire	♐	♒, ♎	♓, ♍	♈, ♌	♉, ♋	♊
Cardinal Earth	♑	♓, ♏	♈, ♎	♉, ♍	♊, ♌	♋
Fixed Air	♒	♈, ♐	♉, ♏	♊, ♎	♋, ♍	♌
Mutable Water	♓	♉, ♑	♊, ♐	♋, ♏	♌, ♎	♍

ogy conference sticks a chart in your face and expects you to say more than, "Hmmmm." What if that someone turns out to be *someone*, and you need to know, on the spot, what contacts their planets make to yours? Or, as once happened to me, what if you're in an ambulance speeding to a hospital, dazed, but gamely trying to figure out which transit caused that car accident.

Table 1 also gives each aspect's suggested orb (the number of degrees allowed on each side of the exact aspect). For instance, a sextile's orb is 2 to 4 degrees. Therefore, any sextiles to a planet at 8 degrees of Aries would be found between 4 and 12 degrees of Gemini and between 4 and 12 degrees of Aquarius. Using this method, however, you would sometimes extend orbs past the software's default settings, particularly for the Sun or Moon. For this and other reasons, you are better off drawing the aspects in manually rather than having the computer draw them.

You should extend orbs for a series of angles to the same planet. Suppose Mercury, Saturn, and Pluto are conjunct, with Jupiter in the opposite sign. Mercury and Saturn are "legally" opposite Jupiter, but Pluto is out of range of an opposition by a degree or two. If you explained the traits of a Jupiter-Pluto opposition to someone, he or she would probably agree that it worked. You should especially extend orbs if the series of angles forms a triangle or rectangle, as in a Grand Trine or T-square, which we call a major configuration. (We'll see examples later.)

You should also allow more orb when a planet forms a wide aspect, but also disposes of the second planet, strengthening the connection. By an old rule, if Venus is in Pisces, then Neptune disposes of Venus, because Neptune rules Pisces. This means that Venus in Pisces is already enough like Neptune that they may be said to be in aspect. Thus, if Venus in Pisces forms a wide square to Neptune, the aspect is stronger than you may expect.

Regarding Jeane Dixon's chart, a question remains in my mind as to whether or not she has a mutable T-square. Pluto in Gemini is closely square Jupiter in Pisces and opposes Uranus in Sagittarius by nearly 8 degrees—perhaps a bit wide for such slow-moving planets. Does Jupiter also aspect Uranus—an 8-degree square—to complete a T-square? It seems quite wide, though Jupiter, as the ruler of Sagittarius, disposes of Uranus. She may have a T-square, and she may not. There are no absolutes.

When questioning whether an aspect is too wide, the final authority is the person who lives with it. Describe its effects, and ask whether it operates in the individual's life. A chronically absent-minded woman I know has a 6-degree square between Mercury and Neptune and no other chart features that explain the chaos in her office or her chronically misplaced keys. Pluto-Mars conjunctions—and their worst-case scenarios—ran in one family with at least three generations of incest. The son had an 8-degree conjunction, as did the father. The paternal grandfather, who set the pattern in motion, had them 10 degrees apart. Repeated examples like these have led me to be generous with orbs.

Another Visual Aid—Drawing in Aspects

As you find the aspects, draw them on the wheel. This clarifies which planets have many aspects and which have few. The most-aspected tend to be high-focus concentrations of energy, while the least-aspected are harder to integrate. Without this visual aid, it is easy to miss major configurations like Grand Trines or Grand Crosses. Bracket conjunctions to distinguish them from planets that are in the same house but not conjunct, or to link planets that are conjunct but in neighboring houses or signs.

Jeane Dixon's natal picture is shown with her aspects in chart 3 (see page 19). Pluto and the Moon are strongly aspected. We may suspect that issues related to the Moon and Pluto were important in her life, though we do not yet know in what ways. Saturn's only major aspects are its conjunctions to Mercury and the Midheaven. We'll look at Mercury-Saturn aspects in detail in the course of this book, so you will get more insight into Dixon's conjunctions as we go along.

Use contrasting colored lines to distinguish between stressful and supportive aspects. For healing purposes, I use pink for hard angles (squares, oppositions, semisquares, and sesquiquadrates) and blue for softer ones (sextiles, trines, and quintiles). With a heavily-aspected point, you'd hope both pink and blue lines were included. A prevalence of pink lines suggests a high-stress life path, while a good supply of blue shows flow and ease to offset harder placements. Almost everyone has more pink than blue—we're not on vacation here!

An exception to this color code is that I mark the quincunx (also called "inconjunct") in something loud, like neon chartreuse. That often-ignored 150-degree angle is a jarring note, especially when the Sun or Moon are involved. This person struggles to reconcile ill-fitting signs, like Scorpio and Gemini, or Leo and Capricorn.

This difficulty is acute with the Eye of God (also known as "Yod" or "Finger of Fate"), made up of two planets quincunx a particular point, but sextile each other. That formation, which appears in Jeane Dixon's chart, is easily missed if the lines aren't drawn. Generally, we might not allow her 4-degree quincunx between Neptune and that angular Venus, except that it completes a Yod. Venus in Sagittarius sextiles Mercury in Aquarius, and both are quincunx Neptune in Cancer. (We will take apart the Yod and other major configurations in chapter seven.)

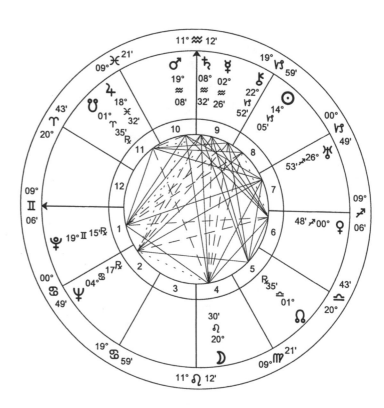

Chart 3. The natal chart of Jeane Dixon, with the aspects drawn in.

Spotting Themes in a Chart

Conducting the overview of a chart, you may begin to see patterns. As you continue to analyze the chart, the patterns may repeat themselves and show up as themes. Regardless of which techniques and tools you choose, major themes will emerge as you go over a chart with great care.

An old astrological rule says that, if you see something once in a chart, it's a potential, twice is a possibility, and three times is a near certainty. For this reason, do not be alarmed—or elated—over a possibility that some chart feature or aspect seems to promise unless you encounter it in several ways. For instance, you might find Pisces on the 7th-house cusp and Venus in the 12th, aspecting Neptune, three placements similar in meaning.

In addition to what you see, pay attention to what you don't see. Factors that are missing or underemphasized are also important, for it can be difficult for the native to use those energies naturally. We've already spoken of empty houses or sectors. You will also want to notice elements that are weak or missing (e.g., the person who has no water), types of aspects that are missing (e.g., no oppositions), and planets that have no aspects, or only minor ones.

In Jeane Dixon's chart, the Sun is remarkable for its near-isolation. It is not strongly aspected—semisquare Venus and very widely sextile Jupiter—nor does it aspect the angles. It is also the only planet in earth, though Saturn—in an air sign—is conjunct the Midheaven. It is important to note when the Sun is unaspected or only weakly integrated, yet this clearly doesn't mean that the person will never amount to much. (John Kennedy's Sun was virtually unaspected.) What this rather strange Capricorn Sun meant in Jeane Dixon's life is something to ponder. We can no longer ask her about it, but one may suspect that there was an unvoiced sense of isolation or alienation, in which she felt invisible, except in a professional capacity.

Be aware that some factors may not really be missing, only hiding. The individual who has no earth, yet has Saturn conjunct the Sun and trine the Ascendant, is well endowed with practical, productive earth qualities. The person with no oppositions, but plenty of planets in Libra, can still see the other person's point of view perfectly well. If Mars is in a weak sign and has no aspects, the qualities of Mars may still be amply present if the Sun, Moon, Ascendant, or several planets are in Aries.

Concluding the Visual Overview

Our initial survey of the wheel provides many questions, but few answers. By highlighting angular planets, looking for concentrations of planetary energy, considering full versus empty houses, and drawing in aspects, you begin to sense what is important—these act like red blinking lights on a dial. The meaning of those blinking lights will gradually emerge as you synthesize the horoscope through the process presented in the remaining chapters.

No method is chiseled in stone. After doing charts for a while—particularly after dissecting a substantial number of them with their owners' input—you start to have an instinct for the features that are important. When you tackle a new chart, key features jump out at you. You drop everything and subject those placements to microscopic examination before going back to the rest. Until that starts to happen, work with the steps suggested here.

CHAPTER TWO

The Sun, Moon, and Ascendant— Working Partners or Family Feud?

The most influential factors in a horoscope are generally the Sun, Moon, and Ascendant. They are, therefore, a good place to begin analyzing a chart. It is tempting to consider them as equal, that is, leaving out for the moment planetary aspects and house positions, to consider that a person with Virgo Sun, Libra Moon, and Sagittarius Rising is a blend of one-third Virgo, one-third Libra, and one-third Sagittarius.

That temptation grows when we note that people with the Sun, Moon, or Ascendant in a given sign behave similarly. Virgo Suns, Virgo Moons, and Virgo Ascendants may overwork and have psychosomatic illnesses, but *why* they overwork, and why they get sick, is another matter. What we will discover as we look deeper is that, however similar the outer *behavior* of these three placements may be, their *motivation* is different. Thus, the impact of the Sun, Moon, and Ascendant on the life path, health, and relationships is also different.

Separating Out the Functions of the Sun

The Sun is the core of our being. Its functions include most of the words that begin with self: the sense of self, self-expression, self-confidence, self-esteem, self-worth, self-development, self-sabotage, self-centeredness, and plain old selfishness. The Sun's sign, house, and aspects give us a sense of who we are and are not, and of our capabilities. In brief, the Sun is our identity. You list your Sun's qualities when you describe yourself as "the kind of person who . . . ." You may recall the popular song by John Lennon that said that life is what happens to you while you're busy making other plans. The part of us that makes those other plans is the Sun.

It is often the father or his equivalents who lend the sense of self and of confidence described by the Sun. In old-time astrology, the Sun represented men, while the Moon represented women. Today, more women are developing and expressing their solar qualities through work and creative pursuits, so this is no longer as true. I feel that women are now more free to express their solar qualities than men are to express their lunar sides. Still, in these transitional generations, we don't have enough maternal/career role models. As a result, the rule about the Sun showing the father's influence is still true for many.

The Ascendant and Our Family Role

A useful idea in understanding the rising sign is that of role. Families assign each member a role and pressure them to perform according to those expectations. This phenomenon is well-documented in literature on dysfunctional families, with offspring playing such roles as the lost soul, the family hero, and the family clown. (A Pisces-Rising individual may be the lost soul, Capricorn Rising may be the family hero, while Gemini Rising may be the family clown.)

Fully functional families also assign roles, though with less rigidity than dysfunctional ones. One child may be designated the popular one; another is labeled the troubled one; and another—often the middle child—may be the prodigal son. The popular one is likely to have air or fire rising—Libra, perhaps, or Leo. Especially in an airy family, the troubled one may have a water sign on the Ascendant, like Scorpio or Cancer. The prodigal son? Probably Aquarius. Could you characterize your own family position in a short phrase, and show how that fits your rising sign or 1st-house planets?

Family roles are not easy to fulfill. They are often filled at great personal cost—for instance, by becoming the family scapegoat. However, even when suffering is involved, the role creates a certain comfort zone. It is familiar. The script is written. You don't have to keep recreating yourself. These scripts grease social wheels and let us know what to expect of each other. They are not inherently negative. They are white lies we tell to get along, though not all Ascendants are equally polite—Aquarius Rising is often downright rude!

Behavior based on the Ascendant can become so automatic that it is stereotyped or compulsive. We begin acting in a certain way to please our parents and fulfill their expectations. You might say that the Ascendant describes what the parent wanted in the way of offspring, as opposed to what they got. All too often, what Mom or Dad wanted was a carbon copy, particularly when the child's rising sign is the same as one parent's Sun sign.

We need the Ascendant. Its implicit disguise protects our easily bruised self-esteem against a world that is too often judgmental and unkind. Without it, at a certain level, we would all be nudists. Most of us need our clothes, however, except in intimate situations. Before maturity, we need the Ascendant's protective covering, just as the pea needs the pod to ripen. The rising sign's traits form a protective shell for the sometimes fragile sense of self represented by the Sun.

We practice our role in our milieu growing up and learn it so well that we take it on the road in adult life. The rising sign give us a disguise—a uniform we wear out in the world—one we can hopefully take off in private. It is not our true self, for that is the Sun, but rather what we lead people to expect of us. The difficulty arises when a person becomes what I call "stuck in the Ascendant" and buries the core self in posturing.

Sun Versus Ascendant

The contrast between the role and the true self is clearest in actors who play a character in a television or movie series. Successful actors assume a character's qualities so consistently that they are in danger of being typecast. Some play their parts so convincingly that the public confuses them with the fictional creation. Leonard Nimoy became so identified with Star Trek's Mr. Spock that he titled his autobiography, *I Am Not Spock.*

We lesser folk can also become overidentified with our roles, to our detriment. We become typecast. People begin to expect us to respond in ways that may not represent our true selves, needs, or feelings. This is especially true when a role assigned to us (the Ascendant) doesn't fit our inner or true self (the Sun). The Sun is the core of our being. When we refer to that core, we say, "At heart, I am . . . ."

Given an Aries Ascendant, a sensitive Pisces man who is a poet at heart might feel hard-pressed to keep up the ultramasculine posturing his family and peers thrust upon him. To avoid disapproval, he may mask his Piscean softness and vulnerability with stereotyped, macho, rough-and-ready acts, perhaps bolstering his confidence through an addiction. With Aries Rising, the Pisces Sun may be in the 12th house. If the Sun is in the

12th house and the next sign is rising, there is often a discrepancy between core and façade. The identity is sacrificed to the role. This is part of why a 12th-house Sun can be difficult.

The rising sign determines the Descendant—the 7th-house cusp, opposite in sign and degree to the Ascendant. The Descendant shows which close associates we attract while playing the roles we learned in childhood. Due to our way of presenting ourselves (the Ascendant), we attract others with complementary behaviors (the Descendant). The person who projects a Virgo Ascendant—"let me fix this mess you've gotten yourself into"—is likely to draw a where-on-earth-did-I-park-the-car Piscean or Neptunian as a partner.

Planets in the 1st house, especially within 10 degrees of the Ascendant, profoundly alter the rising sign. The baby boomer with Leo Rising, but Pluto near the Ascendant, projects more Scorpio than Leo. People born with Saturn near the Ascendant are more Saturnine than any Capricorn Rising. Many with Venus Rising are Venusian to a fault, very concerned with appearance and often quite attractive. Any planet near the Ascendant is powerfully, almost compulsively, projected, so that others see the energies of that planet first.

The rising sign and any 1st-house planets determine how others see us, while the Sun determines how we see ourselves. When the Sun and the rising sign are at odds, we tend to feel misunderstood. If you are a "double"—born around sunrise, with the Sun and rising sign the same—your projection of self is likely to be true to form, so that people see you as you are.

How Well Do the Sun and the Ascendant Work Together?

The Ascendant and the Sun go well together when the signs are harmonious, although an actual aspect (give or take a few degrees) makes them work even more smoothly. Signs that are trine fall within the same element—water to water, air to air, fire to fire, or earth to earth. Signs that are sextile involve complementary elements—earth to water, or fire to air.

When the Ascendant and Sun signs are in harmony, the Ascendant's qualities lend a polish to the self-expression that strengthens confidence and self-esteem. Consider a pair of air signs, Libra and Gemini. Libra Sun's social skills and people connections are enhanced by verbally facile, communicative Gemini Rising. Pair watery Cancer with earthy Taurus. Cancer Sun's need for a rewarding home life is supported by Taurus Rising's down-to-earth, richly sensual approach to basic comforts.

When the Ascendant and Sun signs are in disharmony, an inaccurate image is presented and the person struggles with a sense of being misunderstood and undervalued. A warm, social Leo who yearns to shine can have a hard time doing so with somber, good-fences-make-good-neighbors Capricorn Rising. A Virgo Sun can be downright embarrassed at being saddled with a disorderly Pisces Ascendant. On the other hand, Pisces' compassion can tone down the critical, perfectionistic demands of a Virgo Sun.

Sun and Ascendant placements within the same mode—cardinal to cardinal, fixed to fixed, or mutable to mutable—are more difficult combinations. They are at hard angles to one another and tend to work at cross-purposes. Within those modes they may form a conflictual 90-degree angle called a square—for instance, an ultramodern Aquarius with a conservative Taurus, or a modest Virgo to an immodest Sagittarius. Or, they may be in opposition (180 degrees, or six signs, apart)—for instance, Taurus with Scorpio, or Leo with Aquarius. Not in this series, but even more ill-fitting, is the quincunx, also known as inconjunct, that occurs five signs, or 150 degrees, away. This aspect of incongruity pairs let-it-all-hang-out Gemini with none-of-your-business Scorpio, or dot-every-i Virgo with just-do-it Aries. (We'll spend several chapters on aspects.)

One trap implicit in relying too much on the Ascendant is that we may use it to avoid intimacy. By engaging in the stereotyped behavior of that sign, you fend others off, so no one sees the real you. For example, Scorpio with Gemini Rising may use a line of light patter and constant jokes to keep people from knowing what is going on inside and to add an element of charm to Scorpio's penchant for manipulation. The light-hearted and sometimes light-headed Gemini façade, however, can keep others from understanding how deeply Scorpio feels about things.

A Sun-Ascendant Clash—the Comedienne Roseanne

An example of a clash between the Sun and the Ascendant is shown in the chart of the comedienne, Roseanne (see chart 4, page 30). She has the Sun in Scorpio, Aquarius Rising, and the Moon in Gemini. Not only are her Ascendant and Sun square by sign, her Sun is 4 degrees from an exact square to her Ascendant. Sun-Ascendant squares often show people with a great need to be noticed, who then compulsively project themselves through an image that is at odds with their essential natures.

The Aquarius Ascendant is often a gadfly, tweaking society's sensibilities by outrageous behavior. Consider the time Roseanne and Tom Arnold "mooned" reporters, or the time when she grabbed her crotch and spat after singing the national anthem. These actions may have been very entertaining for her Aquarius, but how did they sit with her self-protective Scorpio? How appalled was her private, even secretive Scorpio when she called yet another press conference and released the latest bombshell about her unconventional relationships?

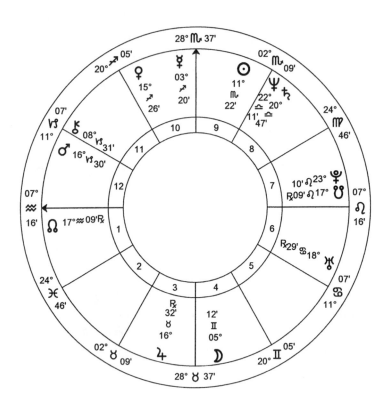

Chart 4. Roseanne. Lois Rodden's DataNews, *#29, gives her birth data, from the birth certificate, as November 3, 1952, 1:21 P.M. MST, in Salt Lake City, UT, 111W53; 40N45. The chart is shown in the tropical zodiac, using Placidus houses.*

Talk about mixed messages—Scorpio needs to control, while Aquarius rebels at the slightest hint of control and strives for freedom at all costs. One week she announces that she and Tom Arnold are both marrying his sexy young assistant. The next, she fires the secretary and divorces Tom because he is having an affair with the secretary. It all makes for fabulous press coverage, but what about personal happiness? I think not.

What accounts for Roseanne's enduring popularity? Why has she not been pilloried for daring to be a rebel? She gets away with it, in part, because of her humor, verbal skills, and intelligence—qualities that air signs like Aquarius and Gemini have in abundance. Her Aquarius Ascendant trines her Gemini Moon and sextiles Mercury. With trines to the Ascendant by the Sun or Moon, we can get away with showing substantial parts of ourselves to the world. We find acceptable, and even likable, ways to reveal our true selves (Sun) or our feelings and needs (Moon).

Bringing the Moon into the Picture

The Moon is the imprint of our mothers or mother figures. It represents part of us that begins to develop in infancy, in our mothers' arms, before we have any verbal capacity. At that age, we do not understand who we are (the Sun) or how we fit into the family (the Ascendant). We only know what we feel—hunger, heat, cold, dampness, rage, fear, or need. The Moon is our sense of comfort and safety, or lack of it. The Sun develops later and is more conscious and verbal. One must have a sense of self as separate from caretakers before a self-concept can develop.

It is difficult to summarize all that the Moon represents. I've written not one, but two entire tomes on the subject. (Readers interested in covering this topic in depth may wish to consult my books, *The Moon in Your Life* (York Beach, ME: Samuel Weiser, 1996), or *Moon Signs* (New York: Ballantine, 1989). We learn about the lunar areas of life from our mothers and their equivalents. With many men now taking part in child care, it will be interesting to see how the charts of children brought up by male caretakers will reflect that lifestyle.

Maternal programming determines which emotions we are comfortable expressing, what we do to make ourselves feel secure, our model for nurturing ourselves and others, and with what kinds of women we surround ourselves or what kind we strive to be. A child with Moon in Capricorn or a Moon-Saturn aspect is often born to a mother with one or more of the following characteristics. She may be older, anxious, depressed, overwhelmed with responsibilities, or strongly career oriented. The offspring of women who suffer deep postpartum depressions often have placements like these. If a mother is chronically depressed, her infant soaks up her sadness, and depression can become a keynote in the child's adult life. If Mom perpetually worries about financial security and experiences hardship, the child may come to view the world as unsafe and act accordingly.

How the Moon and Ascendant Relate to One Another

You may have difficulty separating the Ascendant from the Moon. The family teaches us about both, but at slightly different stages of our development. The Moon—the maternal imprint—happens before the child has enough mental development to know that there is a role to be played (the Ascendant). It happens even before it is entirely clear that child and parent are separate (the Sun). Before we have words for it, we learn whether the world is safe or not. We also soak up our mothers' typical emotions, and they predominate in our own emotional makeup.

We spoke of the Ascendant as the role we play in the family, showing how we need to behave to survive our early environment. Though these three factors continue to unfold throughout life, the core qualities of the Moon and Sun are both formed earlier than the Ascendant. To grasp the role family members train us to play, we need at least a rudimentary social sense. (We first need a sense of ourselves as separate, which is the Sun's domain.) We need to know that each person in the family has a part to play, as well as what is expected of us within that family economy. Although the part can become "knee-jerk" and automatic, it can take much of our childhood to perfect. The Ascendant is social conditioning and generally conscious, whereas the Moon is much less conscious.

When the Ascendant and Moon signs are complementary, they can collude to protect us from showing too much vulnerability (e.g., being too insecure and needy, or too openly emotional). Such patterns strengthen our armor—a vital factor for surviving in the world, not necessarily a drawback. However, when we cover our feelings and needs too rigidly, relationships become less than authentic. We also risk psychosomatic illness—another reason the Ascendant and 1st-house planets show physical vulnerabilities.

Even in mismatched signs, the Ascendant can aid and abet the Moon in avoiding feelings. Imagine the combination of tough-it-out Aries Rising and work-until-you-drop Virgo Moon. Neither sign offers the native any slack. The result can be a driven individual, on the go, until pole-axed by illness or exhaustion.

The Ascendant shows how we hide lunar needs or seduce others into meeting them. Having the two signs in harmony enhances the chances of having needs met without great striving. Take Cancer and Pisces, two signs that are trine, as an example. Cancer Moon often has a strong residue of dependency—

however strongly it may be hidden by compulsively nurturing others. Add a Pisces Ascendant, and the person may assume a confused, helpless pose that entices others to take over (notably Virgos, the sign on the 7th-house cusp). The trine can be a greased slide. Lacking a support system, people with this combination can fall prey to eating disorders or other addictions to soothe their emotions. However, the combination can also produce an extremely compassionate, nurturing individual, one you would want around you in times of grief.

Suppose the two factions are in disharmony (e.g., a timid and even clinging Cancer Moon paired with a ruggedly independent Aquarius Ascendant). Then the facade works against meeting dependency and security needs. Conscious effort is then required to express and meet needs. Imagine the frustration of a Libra Moon with Capricorn Rising. Libra Moons, above all, want to do everything with the approval and participation of their significant others. Capricorn Rising was raised to tough it out alone, organizing every facet of life so perfectly that he or she needs not rely on anyone. Or, suppose a Sagittarius Moon has Taurus Rising. The fixed, slow-moving, and rather rigid approach to everyday life of a Taurus Ascendant may give a restless, vivacious Sagittarius Moon conniptions.

Pairing the Sun and Moon

In studying Sun-Moon combinations, we are, of course working with the phases of the Moon's monthly orbit. No one has done this with as much profundity as Dane Rudhyar, in *The Lunation Cycle* (Santa Fe, NM: Aurora Press, 1986). The material he covers is beyond our scope, but I recommend Rudhyar's book for deeper understanding of Sun-Moon aspects.

When the Sun and Moon signs are harmonious, there is ease between them. What the Sun requires for self-confidence, the Moon easily and instinctively provides. What the Moon needs for security and well-being, the Sun knows how to create. Unless difficult planetary aspects intervene, there is an ease between the male and female parts of the self and an instinctive understanding of the opposite sex. This ease of understanding generally arises from the model of a good relationship between the mother (Moon) and the father (Sun).

When the Sun and Moon are not in harmony, the emotions and needs become what psychologists call ego-alien, meaning that the ego has a hard time reconciling them as a part of itself. ("I shouldn't need that. I'm too . . ." —too strong, too rational, too whatever.)

Consider the inner discomfort of an Aries Sun who has Moon in Cancer. A real-men-don't-wear-galoshes Aries is irked and humiliated by the perceived weakness and insecurity of the Cancer Moon. That Moon goes on a trip and insists on lugging along, not only galoshes, but a canister of the same tea Mom always served back home. The cautious, crablike Cancer, on the other hand, is terrorized and appalled by Aries Sun's rash actions. Aries quits that secure but boring job just when the pension plan is building up to something substantial.

Similarly, an overly intellectual Aquarius Sun views his Pisces Moon as irrational and illogical, with emotions all over the map. The empathic and caring Pisces Moon, however, wishes Aquarius wouldn't be so terribly detached, and even cold, toward the family, especially poor Mom.

Combining Sun, Moon, and Ascendant

We began by saying that people with the Sun, Moon, or Ascendant in a given sign may behave similarly, but with quite different motivations. As we noted, a Virgo Sun, a Virgo Moon, and a Virgo Ascendant may each overwork. Virgo Suns overwork because self-esteem depends on productivity and doing each task more perfectly than others. Virgo Moons overwork because a job well done makes them feel secure in a world they perceive as demanding perfection to remain safe. Being busy also keeps unwelcome emotions at bay. Some Virgo Ascendants overwork because the family cast them as the serving wench, the Cinderella who was left at home while the lazy, undeserving stepsisters went to the ball. (This description is oversimplified, but a full delineation, with all those particulars Virgos love, would require a chapter in itself!)

Capricorn Suns, Moons, and Ascendants all strive for success, but for different reasons. The Capricorn Moons push to succeed to make the world a safe place—literally to ensure a roof over their heads, and probably Mom's as well, as she grows older. Often the firstborn, Capricorn Risings may climb that ladder because of being cast in the role of family hero. They are given the task of distinguishing or legitimizing the family through worldly accomplishments. People with Capricorn Suns need success for their self-worth and for the parental approval their self-worth requires. Such approval is often fleeting—their parents' demands for achievement tend to escalate with each success. Where once a single A on the report card merited a "well done," the Dean's list soon becomes a minimum requirement.

Now that we have described all three parts, how can you understand them in combination? One method is to picture the Sun, Moon, and Ascendant as a trio of people, each with a part to play in the whole, but with its own personality and agenda. See what alliances and antipathies they form, reflecting the degree of compatibility between the signs involved.

When the Moon and Ascendant are in cahoots, but the Sun sign is odd man out, the developing self can get lost. Suppose the Sun and Ascendant are harmonious, but the Moon is at odds or unrelated. Then the façade supports the ego and self-development, but security needs and emotional expression take a back seat. If the Sun and Moon are mutually supportive, but the Ascendant is dissimilar, there can be an inner harmony not reflected by the image the world has of the person.

Harking back to our discussion of the Gauquelin sectors, when the Sun or Moon fall into one of these, especially if close to the Ascendant or Midheaven, that placement tends to overwhelm the other two. They are no less important to wholeness, mind you, but the angular planet is more obvious to the world and more compulsively acted upon. If the angular planet is the Sun, then the needs of the Moon for security, nurturing, and emotional integration take a back seat to the ego and self-expression needs of the Sun. If the Moon is on the angle, the Sun and its concerns recede into the background. (In daylight, it is hard to see the moon clearly; we only get moonlight when the sun has set.)

Astrodrama is a delightful technique for exploring how the trio works together. Ask one person to play the Sun sign, another to take on the qualities of the Moon sign, and a third to portray the Ascendant. (If you have no astrological playmates, take all three parts in turn or write out the dialogue.) Put them into a typical life situation and see how each reacts. Imagine, for instance, this tripartite person is going to a job interview. The applicant is overeducated for the position, but needs employment badly. Imagine that the prospective employee has Sun in Aquarius, Moon in Cancer, and (fortunately, for the interview outcome), Capricorn Rising. With the ego at stake, the elitist and rebellious Aquarian Sun may be disdainful of the job and convinced the person in charge is no Einstein. The Moon in Cancer is worried sick because the rent is overdue and the dreaded word "eviction" has crossed the landlord's lips. Sun and Moon arrive at the interview barely on speaking terms.

Capricorn Rising covers up the internal strife and puts the best foot forward, coming across as capable, reliable, and conscientious. The CEO hires Cap Rising, then is sooooo shocked when Aquarius Sun shows up for work—although only intermittently and often half an hour late.

A Trio in Harmony—Candice Bergen

An example of someone with the Sun, Moon, and Ascendant in the same element, and thus in harmony, is Candice Bergen. She has Sun in Taurus, Moon in Virgo, and Capricorn Rising (see chart 5, page 39).

Women with strong earth tend to have an earthy charm and staying power—especially Taurus Suns like Candice, Katherine Hepburn and Carol Burnett, all of whom have aged so marvelously. In a woman's chart, the Moon has to do with the subject's vision of what it means to be a woman. With Candice's Virgo Moon and Taurus Sun, earthy qualities greatly strengthen her appeal.

Candice's Sun and Moon are closely trine, meaning that the sense of self enhances the expression of emotions and needs, and vice versa. A supportive connection with her father, ventriloquist Edgar Bergen, is also represented by that trine to the Sun. Trines are lucky, and she admits she was virtually handed her first several film roles because of her dad.

Nonetheless, the Virgo Moon and Capricorn Rising show her to be hardworking and perfectionistic. Building on these early breaks, she went on to carve out a valid place for herself as an actress and comedienne. Richly gifted with the excellent business sense and craftsmanship of the earth signs, Bergen has been a working and successful actress for most of her adult life. Her sitcom, "Murphy Brown," was popular throughout its nine

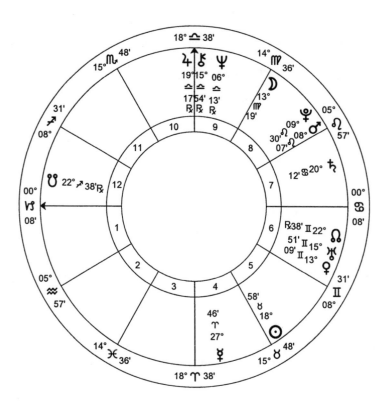

Chart 5. Candice Bergen. According to her birth certificate, she was born May 9, 1946; 9:52 P.M. PST; in Los Angeles, CA; 118W15; 34N04. Cited in Lois Rodden's ASTRO-DATA III *(Tempe, AZ: American Federation of Astrologers, 1986). The information about her life is taken from her autobiography,* Knock Wood *(New York: Ballantine Books, 1985). The chart is shown in the tropical zodiac, using Placidus houses.*

seasons. While her early advantages may be enviable, she has more than earned her ultimate success.

How Aspects Change the Big Three

Aspects, as major modifiers of the Sun, Moon, and Ascendant, introduce another level of complexity. Planets aspecting them (especially conjunctions, when the two planets stand side by side) are so important that they override sign placements. One student bemoaned the lack of water signs in her chart, indicating a supposed lack of emotions. Pluto was conjunct her Ascendant, and Neptune was on her Moon. How emotionless is that?

Planets that modify the Big Three contribute to the skepticism of many who know little about astrology. Imagine a Virgo with hazy, haven't-a-clue Neptune 1 degree from his or her Sun. Try telling this person that Virgos are grounded, orderly, practical, and focused on detail. He or she wouldn't relate to that description at all—and would tell you so in no uncertain terms. Imagine a formerly abused, alienated woman with a 12th-house Leo Moon conjunct Pluto. Just try to tell her that female Leo Moons are Little Mary Sunshines and accomplished hostesses. Not with that Moon! Generalizations that ignore aspects make disbelievers of many people.

Any planet that forms hard angles to more than one of the Big Three is strong, for it colors the person's basic nature. If Saturn opposes the Sun and squares the Ascendant, this can make for a rather Saturnine type, even with nothing in Capricorn. Add planets in Capricorn, plus some in the 10th house (both related to Saturn), and Saturn's traits and issues become a keynote. A supposedly "party hearty" Gemini with these placements may be driven, perfectionistic, goal-centered, anxious, and sometimes depressed. We will learn more about aspects in future chapters, but for now, keep in mind that they must be added to the mix.

Clarifying These Differences Through Transits

Another way of contrasting the Sun, Moon, and Ascendant is to observe what happens when they are transited by the outer planets—Saturn, Chiron, Uranus, Neptune, or Pluto. All such transits coincide with major changes. What facet of the individual is altered, however, depends on which of the Big Three is involved.

When an outer planet transits the Ascendant, we tend to get sick of our roles and break out of them. Take, for example, those with Libra Rising who had transiting Neptune in Capricorn squaring the Ascendant. Many were raised in homes where they took on the role of buffer to warring factions. They grew up as mediators or peacemakers and automatically assumed—or even sought out—that position in conflicts in adult life. No matter how false to their nature that mediation might have been, Libra Rising people who fit that pattern contorted themselves to get along.

Given the transiting Neptune square—or the coming trine from Uranus in Aquarius—the Libra Rising people grow tired of being peacemakers and say, "No more Mr. Nice Guy." (During the Uranus trine, it may be easier to make a statement about who they really are, with that Libra charm to soften it.)

During Saturn's transit of Aries, some Aries-Rising individuals, long entrenched in the leader/trailbreaker role, may decide it is no longer cost-effective to always be out on a limb. Maybe they no longer want to be the brave, strong hero. Maybe they are tired and feeling too old to be forever young. Some may learn the great karmic lesson of Saturn in Aries: Don't go off half-cocked.

People with Aries Suns and Moons may come to the same conclusions. However, with Aries Rising, that pumped-up hero routine was probably always a pose, one they needed for approval or harmony in the family. Dad probably wanted a football captain—and Heaven help the inner poet. Depending on how well the rest of the chart supports it, that fearless mask is difficult to sustain, and, with this transit, it can simply become too much.

As Saturn continues through the 1st house, those lifelong I'm-tough-I-can-take-it Aries defenses and reckless behaviors may finally take their toll on the body. The Ascendant is a health point. Sometimes it is the body that says no for us, when we can't say it ourselves. Here, it may say: "Been there, done that. Won't play that role any more. "

Over the past decade, a similar process has been evident with Capricorn-Rising people as Neptune transited the Ascendant and 1st house. For many, the role in life had been as the responsible one who strove against all hardship to achieve— the CEO of all they survey.

The long struggle to present a perfect façade, to appear totally capable and competent, wore many of these hard-working folks down. They found themselves physically and emotionally unable to continue overproducing. Many of my clients with Chronic Fatigue Syndrome were former Cap-Rising paragons. In illness, they found the only excuse acceptable to their inner parents, the only shelter from a brutally demanding lifestyle.

Not all transits to the Ascendant or 1st-house planets bring on health problems. However, they are a signal to get out from under false roles that are alien to the true self. The health risk comes when we knuckle under to pressure and persist in acting a part for which we're not suited—or have even come to detest.

When a planet that has transited the 12th house for some time crosses the Ascendant, we see major shifts in ways of interacting with significant others. The outer change is the culmination of an underground, inner process (12th house) that resulted in an unwillingness and even an inability, to continue in that old role.

Transits to the Sun—Redefining the Core Self

In contrast to the way the Ascendant evolves, transits to the Sun represent identity crises in which we reconsider who we are. Sometimes we are chastened—as when we realize that we aren't living up to our standards and ideals. Sometimes we are pleasantly surprised to find we've been downplaying our strengths and abilities and are capable of much more than we thought. Sometimes we discover both of the above in turn, during a two-year or longer outer-planet transit to the Sun.

As the transit proceeds, we discard an outgrown self-concept in favor of one that reflects our personal evolution—or devolution. This is often the case with Saturn aspects to the Sun, in which we encounter challenging situations that stretch us and ask us to live up to our potentials. While Saturn is transiting a sign, individuals with that Sun sign commonly emerge into prominence.

People having Pluto transits to the Sun, such as Sagittarians and Geminis currently face, shed the less desirable or evolved traits of their signs and transform to a higher level of evolution of the sign. The ego may be assaulted, only to be revealed as a false self-concept. The dross is purified through obsessive self-examination and, at the end of the process, there is an empowerment of the true or core self, with richer self-expression. (We'll hear more about outer-planet transits as we go along.)

Women having major transits to the Sun often go through a crisis with the men in their lives, thinking they, too, have to change. They become frustrated that the men aren't *more*. More *what* doesn't particularly matter. They should just be *more*. Hopefully, rather than just changing partners in the dance of life, a woman going through this passage comes to see that the one who needs to change, who needs to be *more*, is herself. It is, after all, her Sun that is being transited. And it is her own solar core that is stirring—her need for self-expression.

Resistance to growth, the inertia that dampens the life force, and the feminine programming, make her project the need for growth onto the partner. If only he were *more*, he would save her from the need for fuller self-development. The problem with looking for a new man is that once the Sun begins to stir, no man will measure up for her any longer. She must do it for herself, or her self-esteem—and his—will suffer.

And, yes, if you're wondering, when a man goes through an outer-planet transit to his Moon, he goes through an analogous process with the key woman or women in his life. There is strife because he wants her to be more lunar—more nurturing, more sheltering, a better Mom. What he really needs is to incorporate more of his own lunar qualities.

Moon Transits—Crossing Lunar Thresholds

A long chapter in *The Moon in Your Life* is devoted to outer-planet transits to the birth Moon. Briefly, such transits herald important transitions in lunar areas of life. These areas include the home and roots, mother and your tie to her, nurturing, food, key women in your life, the feminine reproductive cycle, and your way of dealing with emotions. I call these changes lunar thresholds, because crossing them alters your foundations, making you readjust on a deeply emotional level.

The exact nature of the lunar threshold depends on the stage of life. Take the connection between female physiology and the Moon. For a pre-teen girl, a lunar transit may accompany the onset of menstruation. For a young adult woman, it may mean motherhood. For a 50-year-old woman, it may usher in menopause.

The Moon also represents your roots. As a young adult, you may leave the family home under a Moon transit and establish a new home on your own. In your 40s or 50s, a lunar transit may mean that your children are growing up and moving out. In your 60s, such an aspect may come when you retire and move from what has been home to a warmer climate or a small, more manageable apartment.

These are only two of many ways transits to the Moon manifest. They tend to affect several lunar areas of life at once, since the Moon's functions are so interdependent that a shift in one stimulates change in others. Suppose transiting Uranus aspects your Moon, and you are a young adult moving away from your home town. The urge to move is a signal that you have reached a new level of maturity in which you are no longer as dependent on your family. At the same time, living far away from home forces you to grow up even more.

It also alters your relationship with your mother. Like it or not, you are now more equal, and, if she wants to maintain a meaningful relationship, she has to begin treating you as a friend and peer. Sometimes, instead, the impetus for growth comes from her. She refuses to enable you any longer and insists that you stand on your own two feet. Whether the demand comes from without or within, the result is the same—a new level of independence.

CHAPTER THREE

Plugging in the Individual Planets

Now that we see the relative importance of the Sun, Moon, and Ascendant, let's get clear about the other planets. Each has a separate and distinct set of functions in the psyche, and, to be whole and healthy, we need them all. The planets have many levels of meanings from the most trivial to the most profound. Mercury's condition in your chart governs matters as diverse as whether your penmanship is legible and what your chances are for becoming a writer in this lifetime. The Moon shows character patterns ranging from whether you overindulge at buffets to how you might react when your mother dies. Mars shows everything from whether you'd cheat to win at cards to how likely it is that you'd run into a burning building to save a child.

The planets are an inexhaustible well of information about the human psyche. There is no way any book could cover all their levels. They are profoundly modified by their sign and house placements. Many good texts describe each planet in all twelve signs and all twelve houses. So that you're not confined to memorizing what others have written, my goal is to teach you to develop your own descriptions and, eventually, to integrate planet, sign, and house.

Step One: Dismantling the Sign

The first step in this process is to spell out the generic qualities of the sign. Two important facets are its element (fire, earth, air, or water) and its mode (cardinal, fixed, or mutable). We won't cover these divisions in detail, though we will take them into account later in discussing aspects. If your fluency with the elements and modes is still limited, study and meditate on them to deepen your knowledge of the signs. This can also enhance your grasp of relationships between various signs—for example, why Aries (cardinal fire) clashes with Capricorn (cardinal earth).

Combining element and mode is one way to figure out a sign's nature. Leo is fixed fire, evoking the eternal flame or endless sunshine. Taurus is fixed earth—stubborn and stodgy, yet forever fruitful. Gemini is mutable air, suggesting diverse interests and a gift of gab. For a deeper sense of how mode and element shape a sign, contrast signs within an element. Think about how fixed fire (Leo) differs from cardinal fire (Aries) and from mutable fire (Sagittarius).

You can gain another helpful perspective from Dr. Zipporah Dobyns' "alphabet," based on shared qualities of equivalent planets, signs, and houses. Leo, for instance, is intrinsically related to the Sun and to the 5th house, so its concerns are similar to theirs. Libra is connected with the 7th house and Venus, and they all share certain functions and issues. Saturn is like Capricorn in spades. The matters of the 10th house, which describes career, achievements, and authority figures, are important to both Capricorns and heavily Saturnian people. For a more detailed explanation of this meaty system, read Dr. Dobyns' books.

I subscribe fundamentally to this line of thought, but make exceptions where the houses do not seem so much like the associated sign or planet. No doubt these are merely semantic differences, for Dr. Dobyns' insights contribute greatly to making astrology easy to learn. As an example of where we diverge, I don't equate 1st-house planets with Mars. Although they can be as forcefully and energetically expressed as Mars, they have little connection with such major Martian domains as anger, competition, and sexual expression.

Planets in the 1st house, especially near the Ascendant, are so like themselves as to be overpowering. They are right out front for the native and everyone he or she encounters to trip over. An individual with Uranus near the Ascendant can "out-eccentric" any Aquarian. Having the Moon within 10 degrees of the Ascendant, whether in the 1st or the 12th, makes the person extremely lunar. Therefore, such people can be highly emotional and project either nurturing or the need to be nurtured. Naturally, the Moon sign has to be considered, for an Aquarian Moon would not fit this pattern. However, the Moon is so powerful in this position that it can virtually derail whatever life path the Sun wants to pursue.

Another exception is that those who have Taurus and the 2nd house strong don't seem like Venus, but like the earth herself. People with a strong Venus act more like airy, relationship-focused, people-pleasing Librans than like earthy, financially savvy, stubborn Taurians. Similarly, those with Mercury conjunct the Sun or Ascendant behave like ultra-Geminian types— chatty, flighty, and scattered—not like organized, detail-oriented, critical Virgos. The word "mercurial" doesn't describe the well-grounded sign of Virgo. I am not alone in leaving open the rulerships of Taurus and Virgo. (In the next chapter, we will consider how a planet becomes strong.)

How Planets Are Affected by Their Signs

In describing a planet in a sign, you can't just repeat the Sun-sign description. Consider how that particular planet mixes with the sign. Ponder, for instance, how Venus in Scorpio is different from Mercury in Scorpio and from Moon in Scorpio. To answer that question, blend the issues, concerns, or functions of the planet with the traits of the sign.

Start by brainstorming to make a generic list of traits for Scorpio. Given Pluto's rulership of Scorpio, some of Pluto's issues—like power and its uses, transformation, and healing—preoccupy Scorpio natives. The related house (the 8th) pertains to birth, death, sex, and other people's resources. Combining house and planet, we can guess that strongly Scorpionic people are often fascinated with death, birth, sexuality, power, betrayals of trust, transformation, the occult, and healing. It is a fixed water sign, so it is intensely emotional and holds onto those feelings for long periods.

When you've come up with a list of traits, look back at your texts and notes to see if you're on the right track, and add more if necessary. Descriptions of Scorpio go on for pages. They include positive potentials like depth, perceptiveness, analysis, focus, and endurance. They also include negative characteristics like vindictiveness, jealousy, possessiveness, and manipulation. Whether a Scorpio expresses higher-level traits or lower ones is a matter of individual evolution. This can't be seen in the chart.

Venus is concerned with love, so people with Venus in Scorpio may act Scorpionic when they are in love—i.e., possessive, obsessive, intense, and mistrustful toward lovers or mates.

Mercury represents the mind, so Mercury in Scorpio thinks in a Scorpionic way. When confronted with a puzzling situation or learning challenge, these types go off by themselves and think deeply, analyze, or even brood over the matter until it is resolved. The Moon rules issues like home, family, and security, so Scorpio Moons can sting like a scorpion when their paramount concerns are threatened.

From Keywords to Descriptions

A helpful approach to planetary descriptions is to make separate lists of keywords and phrases associated with that planet and that sign. Suppose you are considering Mercury in Aquarius. What role does Mercury play in the chart and what functions and concerns are assigned to it? What personality traits are associated with Aquarius?

Mix and match items in the two lists to see how Mercury operates in Aquarius. Among other things, Mercury rules ideas, thinking, communicating, perception, persuasion, humor, and manual dexterity. Aquarius is a fixed air sign associated with the 11th house and the planet Uranus. Adjectives used to describe Aquarius are brilliant, innovative, inventive, unusual, eccentric, nonconforming, shocking, contrary, rebellious, iconoclastic, visionary, and humanitarian.

Blending keyword lists, we come up with some ways Mercury's energy might be expressed in Aquarius (see table 2, page 52).

There are dozens of possible expressions, and a given individual with this placement won't share them all. Not every Mercury in Aquarius child grows up to earn a Ph.D. in science; just as many drop out of school and become bikers. They rebel against the educational system's demands to conform and to regurgitate what the texts say. These are two extremes, and

Table 2: Mercury and Aquarius Blended.

MERCURY	AQUARIUS	MERCURY IN AQUARIUS
Thinking	Brilliant, innovative	Brilliant new ideas
Perceptions	Eccentric	Oddball perspectives
Communication	Shocking, rebellious	"In your face" style
Humor	Unusual, offbeat	Zany, wacko humor
Persuasion	Humanitarian	Good advocate
Dexterity	Inventive	Inventor, engineer

plenty of these types fall in the middle—perhaps studying astrology or computers.

Make keyword lists for your own Mercury sign and match them up with Mercury's functions to see how that list differs from Mercury in Aquarius. If your Mercury is in vivid, dramatic, but opinionated Leo, your thinking will take on that coloration. If it is in optimistic, philosophical, but often-meandering Sagittarius, that shapes your mental outlook as well. If it is in peace-loving, charming, but indecisive Libra, those traits modify your communication patterns.

Going Deeper: Making a List of Planetary Functions

Keyword lists are an important step toward understanding how the sign modifies the planet. These descriptions focus on externals, however, and lend little insight into motivations for our behavior and interactions with the world. For a psychological portrait of planet in sign, start by making a list of functions, with Pluto as an example. If the original list you come up with is random, work to arrange it into a coherent progression of related ideas, as shown in the partial list that follows.

Functions or Issues of Pluto

What models of power we had;
How we handle our own power;
Where our trust was betrayed;
What we can't forgive;
What we can't let go of;
How we handle grief or loss;
How we protect our secret selves;
How we delve into the hidden;
How we heal ourselves.

In a particular chart, the questions this list raises can be complex. Pluto's house and aspects contain some answers—who taught us to mistrust others and what we cannot forgive for instance. We will learn how the house modifies the planet later in this chapter. Aspects will be the focus of several upcoming chapters.

We get less personal information from the signs of Pluto, Uranus, and Neptune. We call the outer planets' signs "generational placements" because they are in effect for whole generations of births. Slow-moving Pluto remains in a sign eleven years and sometimes more. The group born between 1937 and 1958 exhibits the traits of obsessive Pluto in narcissistic Leo and has been dubbed the "Me Generation." The Pluto-in-Virgo generation, born between 1958 and 1971, has a very different psychology, one we are only beginning to fathom.

Though traditionally called "impersonal," Pluto, Uranus, and Neptune are no less important than the personal planets. This part of the character structure arises from that generation's cultural and historical background—the impact of the era on those growing in it. For instance, those born with Pluto in Cancer grew up during the Great Depression. Throughout their lives, many of them were driven by psychological remnants of that era's mass hunger and insecurity about meeting basic needs.

I have discussed the outer planets' signs in other books, as have several of my gifted colleagues. A satisfying examination of generational placements for Pluto, Uranus, and Neptune would take us too far afield to be useful here. If you are curious about these placements, the techniques in this chapter and the next should make it possible for you to delineate them for yourself.

Integrating Function and Sign

Just as each planet has a set of functions, each sign has a set of character traits. Combining planetary functions with the traits of the sign leads to a profile of how the planet operates in a sign. Let's use Jupiter in Scorpio as an example.

We tend to think of Jupiter as a great big traveling uncle who comes home from time to time with goodies he picked up for us on his trips. I'm not convinced Jupiter is so wonderful. In fact, the so-called "greater benefic" has its shadow side as well. It describes belief systems and, as such, is the root of established religions, with their killing crusades to convert the unbeliever. Religion aside, it is the root of all the "isms" over which mankind has waged war throughout history. With its greed for more and ever more, it is the motivation behind the expansion-ism that is choking Earth and devastating our natural resources. On a personal level, our "isms" and greed for more can get us into considerable difficulty.

To combine Jupiter and Scorpio, first identify Jupiter's functions in the chart. Among other things, it describes:

Functions of Jupiter

The philosophy of life you espouse;
Spiritual practices that appeal;
How you educate yourself;
Where you push your luck;
How you learn from mistakes;
How you seek to grow and expand;
What you can teach others;
Where you find the silver lining.

Match the functions of Jupiter with the traits of Scorpio identified earlier, and see how they blend. Here are a few possible expressions:

Jupiter Functions	*Jupiter's traits in Scorpio*
The philosophy of life you espouse	*Do unto others first;*
Spiritual practices that appeal	*Occult pursuits; tantric sex;*
How you educate yourself	*Solitary, in-depth research;*
Where you push your luck	*Going into debt;*
How you learn from mistakes	*Intense self-analysis;*
How you seek to grow and expand	*Introspection and study;*
What you can teach others	*How to heal the past;*
Where you find the silver lining	*Seldom poor.*

The list is a deliberate mix of uplifting potentials and admittedly less evolved ones. That 8th sign has a range of symbols, from the scorpion, to the eagle, to the phoenix. Just don't glee-fully conclude that the Jupiter in Scorpio you meet at the next astrology conference (or, more to the point, the next Wiccan gathering) will initiate you into tantric sex. He or she is equal-ly likely to turn you into a toad.

How does Jupiter in Scorpio differ from Jupiter in another sign—Capricorn for instance? Begin by writing down what you know about Capricorn, which is similar to Saturn. Capricorn is cardinal earth—fruitful, productive, and goal-oriented. Related to the 10th house, it is highly career-minded.

Balance positive and negative traits. On the positive side, Capricorn tends to be disciplined, reliable, responsible, strong in character, and able to delay gratification for long-term goals. Capricorns can be late bloomers, but they age well, coming into their own in maturity. On the down side, many Capricorns are more often down than up, tending to be depressed, anxious, and overly serious. In their climb up the ladder of success, they have been known to be cold, ruthless, and antisocial.

Consider how this abbreviated list of Capricornian traits could apply to the functions of Jupiter. Then come up with a set of possible expressions, like those below.

Jupiter Functions	*Jupiter in Capricorn*
The philosophy of life you espouse.	*We're not here to play;*
Spiritual practices that appeal . . .	*Monasticism; self-flagellation;*
How you educate yourself.	*The school of hard knocks;*
Where you push your luck.	*Working far too hard;*
How you learn from mistakes. . . .	*Slowly, but surely;*
How you seek to grow and expand	*Climb the ladder to success;*
What you can teach others	*Discipline and quality;*
Where you find the silver lining.	*Life begins at 40.*

The High Road or the Low Road?

Each piece of the chart can have both constructive and destructive uses. Like the goddess Kali, Scorpio and Pluto can represent either a birth or a death in some facet of our lives. Strong placements of Neptune and Pisces can be the hallmark of saints or sinners, or anywhere between. We may guess how the energy of the sign or planet is currently being used, based on placements and aspects. Yet, no one can know for sure by looking at a chart, only by observing and talking to the person. One gift of astrology is the ability to recognize when we are taking the low road and to find higher uses of the same energy.

Let's contrast a single planet in two very different signs, Pisces and Gemini. Pisces is a mutable water sign, so it is emotional, in a diffuse way. It can also adapt to a large variety of conditions, the way water in a stream flows around a rock. It is ruled by Neptune, a planet with a spectacular spread of meanings ranging from spirituality, service, imagination, and creative inspiration on the positive side, to deception, martyrdom, addiction, and self-delusion on the negative side. Pisces is naturally connected with the 12th house, another part of the chart with meanings ranging from the lofty to the self-defeating. That house describes what is unconscious or secret, where we serve others in order to save ourselves, and where we are our own worst enemies. The sign Pisces shares many of the concerns and qualities of its ruler and associated house.

Gemini is a mutable air sign. It makes you think of the wind—light, airy, but continually shifting. Gemini is ruled by Mercury, the planet of communication, writing dexterity, and persuasion, and Geminians tend to be gifted in all these matters. The sign is connected with the 3rd house, which is also concerned with communication. What qualities and traits does Gemini have that arise from these intrinsic sign, house, and rulership relationships?

Table 3 on page 59 depicts the planet Mars as it might operate in both Pisces and Gemini. The first column lists several of Mars' functions. The second shows high-level expressions of that sign; the third shows lower ones. The two poles represent extremes. For individuals with those placements, the true pattern is apt to fall between the two and shift from time to time, or situation to situation.

To understand more about how signs modify planets, compare the Pisces and Gemini lists line by line. Consider, for instance, what makes each of them mad. Mars in Pisces gets upset at man's inhumanity to man, while Mars in Gemini can't abide stupidity. Where leadership is required, Mars in Pisces can be a spiritual warrior, while Mars in Gemini leads the field with avant-garde ideas. At the negative end of the romantic spectrum, neither is the guy Mom or Dad would want their little girl to marry. Considering each function in turn, contrasts between Mars in Pisces and Mars in Gemini become clear.

For more insight into how Pisces and Gemini differ, contrast Venus in the two signs. The first column of table 4 lists a few functions of Venus (see page 60). The second suggests positive uses of that Venus sign; the third shows undesirable ones. Again, the self-awareness that astrology lends can help people progressively let go of less-evolved expressions and choose higher ones.

These are two very different Venuses, and two entirely different patterns of loving. Looking at the positive qualities of Venus in Pisces, you begin to understand why traditional astrologers considered Venus exalted in Pisces.[1] Shaking your

---

[1]Although rather deterministic, this classical system of ranking planets by their signs of exaltation (ideal functioning), detriment (difficult functioning) and fall (worst placement) contains many insights. A planet in its own sign is in domicile and has a particularly strong, unfettered expression of the qualities of the sign and planet. However, each planet in each sign has valid karmic purposes and higher, versus lower, uses.

Table 3. Positive and Negative Expressions of Mars in Pisces and Gemini.

FUNCTIONS OF MARS	MARS IN PISCES +	MARS IN PISCES -	MARS IN GEMINI +	MARS IN GEMINI -
What makes you mad	Cruelty to others	Hasn't a clue	Mental inertia	Stupidity
How anger is handled	Compassionately	Passive-aggressively	Sharply, clearly	Sarcastic, biting
Asserting yourself	Gently, with empathy	"A doormat"	Verbalizing limits	Cuts you to shreds
How you compete	Rises above battle	Fades from challenges	By being the smartest	Talk opponent down
Leadership traits	Spiritual warrior	Serving false gods	Leading-edge ideas	All talk, no action
Directing energy	Fluid, adaptable	Diffuse, unfocused	Mentally charged	Lives in the head
How you "go for it"	Caring about others	Shoot self in foot	Plan an attack	Splitting efforts
Sexual expression	Sensitive, romantic	Impotent or untrue	Simmering dialogue	Charming rake

Table 4. Positive and Negative Expressions of Venus in Pisces and Gemini.

FUNCTIONS OF VENUS	VENUS IN PISCES +	VENUS IN PISCES -	VENUS IN GEMINI +	VENUS IN GEMINI -
Whom or what is loved	The highest in all	Drunks, sinners	The mind of each one	Who's new and "in"
How freely you love	Unconditional love	The more it hurts	Quick to accept	Free, but fleeting
How you express love	Sensitive, romantic	Sentimental, maudlin	Verbally charming	Full of blarney
How you attract love	Helping others	Abasing yourself	Dialogue and wit	Talk the talk
Your sense of beauty	Hazy pastels	Christ on a cross	Light, evanescent	Glitter and fads
Capacity to compromise	Empathic perspective	Allowing abuse	Can see both sides	Never takes a stand
How harmony is sought	Soul accord	Giving in too much	Negotiation	"Yes" you to death

head at the lower expressions, you may wonder how many of them attend Al-Anon. Marveling at the best traits of Venus in Gemini, you may begin to revise the guest list for your next party. Seeing the worst ones, you may drag out the charts of those heartbreaking Don Juans or Juanitas who have loved you and left you.

When we mapped out Pluto's functions earlier, you may have concluded that it's not a nice planet. It's not an easy planet to deal with, for sure, but it's not a bad one, either. Without it, we couldn't heal or transform ourselves, one prerequisite of personal evolution. Likewise, Mars has a bad reputation, since it depicts such difficult human interactions as anger and conflict. Conflict is inevitable at times, given that we all want different things. However, Mars also represents focused energy to attain our desires and goals.

Distilled to its essence, no planet is good or bad, only a necessary part of human experience. Each sign placement has its good uses and its side effects. Similarly, your coffee grinder won't vacuum the rug, but it does turn out that tantalizing brew you love in the morning. Astrology teaches us a way to find constructive uses of each planet, sign, and aspect. In the symphony of the planets, we need every note.

Planets in Houses

The next level to integrate is how a planet's energies work within its house placement. It is important to note that the planet does not operate *only* in matters of that house, but in other areas as well. A 6th-house Scorpio Moon will react in a Plutonian way to anything that threatens security. This is true in many areas of life, not just when employment or health is jeopardized. However, given that it is a 6th-house Moon, there is strong potential for suppressed emotions to come out in psychosomatic illness.

Table 5. *Venus in Pisces in the 6th or 9th House.*

6TH HOUSE MATTERS	VENUS IN PISCES IN 6TH	9TH HOUSE MATTERS	VENUS IN PISCES IN 9TH
Type of work chosen	Serving the poor or unfortunate	Approach to the divine	Adoration and devotion
Orientation toward work	Loving compassion in service	Guiding philosophy	God is love; love thy neighbor
Work habits	Long on love, short on detail	Practices that may appeal	Meditation; sacred dance
Relationships with coworkers	Secret affairs; hopeless crushes	Approach to higher education	Party now, study later
Possible health concerns	Sugar or alcohol abuse	Travel and other cultures	Partners may be foreign

Venus shows who and how you love and is not limited to those encountered in the house where it is placed. With Venus in Virgo in the 5th, you will still be a friend-in-need to family, friends, and coworkers, though your children or romantic interests may take up much of your time. Wherever your heart is engaged, you want to correct or improve loved ones. Though they won't always appreciate it, it is part of how you show your love.

As you might expect from the Dobyns' system, however, house placement does color a planet's expression. For instance, a 4th-house Sun is homey, but may be without the emotionality and insecurity of a Cancer Sun. Likewise, in years of social work in medical settings, I have found that many of my colleagues had strong 6th houses. This may be part of the reason why they chose health careers. Moreover, even when Virgo was not strong in their horoscopes, they had Virgoan traits, like being workaholics or living to serve.

Let's return to Venus in Pisces and consider how it operates in matters of the 6th house, versus concerns of the 9th house. Table 5 includes a mixture of positive and negative ways to express Venus in Pisces, since we function at a variety of levels (see page 62). Again, we can choose to use those energies constructively.

Putting These Techniques to Work

We now have a method for analyzing the planets in a horoscope. We have seen how each is modified by sign and house placements and how each can be put to either positive or negative use. I encourage you to practice these steps and stages on several charts before going on to the next part of the process—the important dimension of planetary aspects. You may note that we seem to neglect or condense some of the steps in succeeding chapters. If we slogged through written analyses of each step for every planet considered, this book would be an epic. In your own studies, however, pursue each step until it becomes second nature.

You may be wondering how you use certain of your natal planets yourself. Do you take the high road as a rule, are you in a rut on that low road, or are you somewhere between? The Moon's monthly orbit around all twelve signs can provide a reality check. Tracking its path around your chart for several months in a row is one way to understand yourself and your natal wheel. As it crosses over each placement, it acts as a cosmic highlighting pen. For those few hours a month, it brings inner dynamics into bold relief. For instance, crossing Mars, it clarifies how you experience and express anger and conflict.

CHAPTER FOUR

What Planet Are You From?

When Edgar Cayce did trance readings, he described subjects' "planetary sojourns"—the planets on which they spent time between incarnations. In most charts, one or more planets are so heavily emphasized that they become keynotes in the individual's life. Like many astrologers, I believe we choose when to be born, for whatever misguided and dimly-remembered reasons, and that every natal chart is, therefore, an election chart. Thus, keynote planets are clues to your most important issues, tasks, and life purposes. First, however, we need to determine which are the keynotes in a given chart. They answer the question: What planet are you from?

How Planets Become Keynotes

Planets are particularly emphasized when they fall into the Gauquelin sectors we discussed in chapter one—i.e., 10 degrees either side of the Ascendant, Midheaven, Descendant, or IC. As you may recall, the Gauquelins' research showed that an individual's most notable or obvious traits matched the qualities of planets in those sectors. Looking back on the charts in chapter two, Roseanne had Mercury in hoof-in-mouth Sagittarius near the Midheaven, and her sassiness is surely memorable. Candice Bergen had Jupiter in Libra in the same area. The image she projects is more elegant and refined, but still humorous and truthful.

A planet is also emphasized when it is one of the most aspected, especially if it aspects more than one of the Big Three. Drawing in aspects provides visual clues as to which planets are strongly aspected and, thus, might be keynotes. If a planet is part of a major configuration, like a Grand Trine, T-square, or Grand Cross, it may be important. (We'll learn how to interpret major configurations in chapter seven.) If there are two such configurations or clusters in a chart, and if one planet is part of both, it is almost certain to be a keynote—for example, if a planet is part of both a T-square and a Grand Trine.

Another help in identifying keynotes is Zipporah Dobyns' "alphabet," the system discussed in the last chapter, that considers related signs, houses, and planets as approximately equal. For instance, if the Sun and Moon are in Sagittarius and there are several planets in the 9th house, Jupiter could be a keynote planet. If Cancer is Rising, the Sun is in the 4th house, and the Moon is heavily aspected, this may be a lunar type. As indicated earlier, I make certain exceptions. These will be reflected in the material that follows.

Table 6 (pages 68-69) is a "cheat sheet" for finding out what planet you come from. To summarize, people strongly exhibit characteristics of a planet when more than one of these conditions are met:

- It aspects one of the Big Three, especially more than one;

- That planet falls into one of the Gauquelin sectors;

- That planet is one of the most aspected in the chart;

- The sign the planet rules contains one of the Big Three or several planets;

- The house connected with the planet contains one of the Big Three or several planets.

This list proceeds from the strongest to the weakest factors. The more of these conditions that apply to a chart, the more that planet typifies the individual. You will probably identify two or more keynotes.

Virgo and Taurus did not find their way into the table, because, as discussed earlier, I do not believe that Mercury rules Virgo or Venus rules Taurus. However, consider yourself from the Virgo home-world (wherever that may be), if you have some combination of the following: one of the Big three or several planets in Virgo, or one of the Big Three or several planets in the 6th house. You are from the Taurus home world (which may just be Earth itself) if any of the following are true: one of the Big Three or several planets are in Taurus, or one of the Big Three or several planets are in the 2nd house.

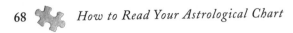

Table 6. E.T. Cheat Sheet: What Planet Are You From?

TYPE	CHARACTERISTICS
SOLAR	One of the Big Three is in Leo • three or more planets are in Leo • the Sun is in the Gauquelin sectors or highly aspected (5th house not entirely true to type).
LUNAR	One of the Big Three is in Cancer or in hard aspect to the Moon • three or more planets are in Cancer • the 4th house contains one of the Big Three or several planets • the Moon is in the Gauquelin sectors, or highly aspected.
MERCURIAL	One of the Big Three is in Gemini or in hard aspect to Mercury • three or more planets are in Gemini • the 3rd house contains one of the Big Three or several planets • Mercury is in the Gauquelin sectors or highly aspected.
VENUSIAN	One of the Big Three is in Libra or in hard aspect to Venus • three or more planets are in Libra • the 7th house contains one of the Big Three or several planets • Venus is in the Gauquelin sectors or highly aspected.
MARTIAN	One of the Big Three is in Aries or in hard aspect to Mars • three or more planets are in Aries • Mars is in the Gauquelin sectors or highly aspected (1st house not true to type).
JUPITERIAN	One of the Big Three is in Sagittarius or in hard aspect to Jupiter • three or more planets are in Sagittarius • the 9th house contains one of the Big Three or several planets • Jupiter is in the Gauquelin sectors or highly aspected.

Table 6. E.T. Cheat Sheet: What Planet Are You From?(cont.)

TYPE	CHARACTERISTICS
SATURNIAN	One of the Big Three is in Capricorn or in hard aspect to Saturn • three or more planets are in Capricorn • the 10th house contains one of the Big Three or several planets • Saturn is in the Gauquelin sectors or highly aspected.
URANIAN	One of the Big Three is in Aquarius or in hard aspect to Uranus • three or more planets are in Aquarius • Uranus is in the Gauquelin sectors or highly aspected • some facets of the 11th house are Aquarian—some are not.
NEPTUNIAN	One of the Big Three is in Pisces or in hard aspect to Neptune • three or more planets are in Pisces • the 12th house contains one of the Big Three or several planets • Neptune is in the Gauquelin sectors or highly aspected.
PLUTONIAN	One of the Big Three is in Scorpio or in hard aspect to Pluto • three or more planets are in Scorpio • the 8th house contains one of the Big Three or several planets • Pluto is in the Gauquelin sectors or highly aspected.
OUTER- PLANET TYPES	When two or three of the outer planets—Uranus, Neptune, and Pluto—are keynote planets by the rules spelled out above, then the individual fits into a special category. I call this individual an Outer-Planet Person (see character description at the end of the chapter).

The Maid from Mercury—Goldie Hawn

It was hard to come up with varied chart examples for this book. Everyone I admired enough—or found interesting enough—to include turned out to be Plutonian. Even lovable ol' Scott Hamilton, the skating sensation, has Pluto conjunct the Sun! Oprah has Pluto on the Ascendant. Whoopi Goldberg has Sun and Moon in Scorpio in the 8th house. My own planetary origins aside, that phenomenon may say something about the power of Plutonians to capture the public imagination.

To show how you find keynote planets, I finally chose Goldie Hawn, whose chart is shown here as chart 6 (on page 71). This enduring and endearing comedienne first delighted us on "Laugh-In" in the late 1960s and has remained a favorite through the 1990s. Despite her zany image, Goldie is not without her Plutonian side, with Sun and Venus in Scorpio, and Pluto aspecting the Moon, Mars, and Venus. However, I would also classify her as a Mercury-Jupiter type, with both those planets in the Gauquelin sectors. Mercury is in the 12th in Sagittarius, but only 7 degrees from the Ascendant. Jupiter is less than 1 degree from the Midheaven, on the 9th-house side that the Gauquelins identified as the most powerful position in the chart. The third planet in a Gauquelin sector is her Gemini Moon, just 1 degree off the Descendant, giving her additional mercurial qualities. Mercury opposes both the Moon and Uranus in Gemini, with Jupiter sextile Mercury and trine Uranus. Are you wondering what it means behaviorally and emotionally to be a Mercury-Jupiter type? Stay tuned!

What the Planetary Types Are Like

Attributes of the planets were once so well-known and accepted that they crept into our language. Webster's *New World*

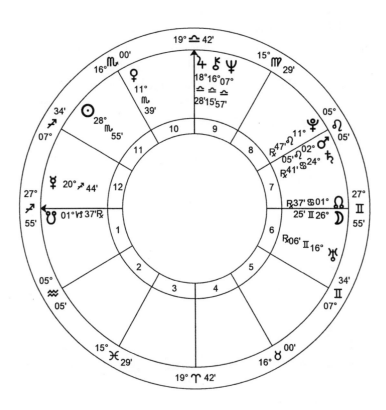

Chart 6. Goldie Hawn. Born 9:20 A.M. on November 21, 1945, Washington, DC, according to the birth record from Contemporary American Horoscope. *The chart is in the tropical zodiac, using Placidus houses.*

Dictionary of the American Language describes a Saturnine individual as one who is sluggish, gloomy, morose, grave, and taciturn—"born under the supposed influence of the planet, Saturn."[1] A Mercurial individual is described as having qualities attributed to the god Mercury or supposedly influenced by the planet Mercury—eloquent, clever, shrewd, thievish, or having qualities suggestive of the metal mercury: quick, quick-witted, volatile, changeable, fickle. The dictionary also defines the Jovial type (ruled by Jupiter), the venial or venereal sin (related to Venus), and the lunatic (affected by the Moon).

Let's look at some brief descriptions of the planetary types. Whole books have been written about each of them and you can consult them if you feel a need to flesh out your understanding.

The Solar Type: This somewhat regal individual has a strong need to shine, to stand out in bold relief, and often does just that. All the *self* words are emphasized: self-expression, self-confidence or self-consciousness, self-development, self-obsession, and even selfishness. At worst, the person can have a big ego and an insatiable need to be noticed, even the center of attention.

The Lunar Type: This is someone who expends much energy tending to lunar concerns. These include nurturing, food, the home, security, women and women's needs, family, and the emotions. The past and family of origin figure strongly in the person's behavior, habits, and emotional issues and are often carried into adult life.

---

[1]Webster's *New World Dictionary of the American Language*, Second College Edition, David B. Guralnik, ed. (New York: Simon and Schuster, 1980). The definition of Saturnine is given on page 1266; Mercurial is defined on page 888.

The Mercurial Type: Here is a natural communicator who would do well to earn a living using those skills. If not channeled into career goals, this energy is squandered on the phone, the Internet, or in incessant chatter. These individuals are restless, changeable, and incurably curious. They don't tolerate boredom well. They are cerebral and even intellectual, and often have a keen sense of humor.

The Venusian Type: For them, relationships are paramount, and they feel unfulfilled without a partner. Romantic, charming, often attractive, if overly concerned with appearance, they hunger for a steady dose of affection and warmth from those around them. Considerate, caring individuals, they often vacillate on decisions because they want to please everyone and keep the peace. They can be too other-directed and thus lack the drive to accomplish things for their own sake.

The Martial Type: These people are action-oriented, often rashly leaping to act before careful thought or planning. They are often seen as leaders because they have abundant energy, drive, zeal, and sureness about their aims. They can be aggressive, hot-headed, or competitive, and lack patience with slower, less certain folks. They are easily irritated, but the sign and aspects of Mars determine how readily they show anger and how it is expressed.

The Jovial Type: This type seeks answers to the big questions of life. In that quest, they tend to be perpetual scholars, whether in formal schooling or self-taught. Once they find an answer they like, they aren't shy about carrying the word enthusiastically to others. Thus, they are often formal or informal teachers, preachers, or public relations people. They can be conventional, moralistic, and preachy, but generous, with a good, though convoluted, sense of humor. Optimistic by nature, they seek to uplift and encourage others and to find lessons in every trial.

The Saturnine Type: This person, early in life, forms strong goals and devotes much of the available time to fulfilling them. Serious, focused, reliable, dutiful, responsible, and capable beyond their years, they can also be somber perfectionists, or depressed and anxious workaholics, especially when stymied in accomplishing their lofty aims. The older they get and the more of their goals they fulfill, the more they grow mellow and give themselves some margin. They can become the elders of the tribe, with valuable practical experience to pass along.

The Uranian Type: These individualists—one might even say characters—abound in eccentricities that can either endear or drive others to distraction. They can rebel when society exerts too much pressure on them to conform to rules that go against their grain. Often advanced in ideas, supportive of social causes, or brilliantly inventive, these folks will often be avant guard, seldom mainstream, though they can start fads. Their beleaguered parents somehow survive a stormy adolescence, during which authority is perpetually questioned. They can be contrary and often discard a workable system simply because it is passé.

The Neptunian Type: Much like the haze that surrounds their signature planet, these beings can be confused and confusing. Their perceptions are less focused on the material world than on realms beyond—the spiritual, the astral, the creative, and the imaginary dimensions. Hard to pin down, they can shift between savior or saved, nurse or patient, saint or sinner, spiritual seeker or lost soul, inspiration or delusion. Some are prone to addictions or fantasies to escape a reality that doesn't fit their dreams. However, they can turn that pattern around. They thus have much to teach all of us in this era of addiction.

The Plutonian Type: Often suffering painful betrayals, losses, and abuses of power in early years, these hawk-eyed observers of humanity, and of life itself, can be wary and mistrustful. Their perceptions are keen, deep, and accurate, yet the conclusions they draw can be distorted by old traumas. Shown a path to healing, they will work obsessively to overcome their own ills or those of others or of society as a whole. Many become therapists, healers, or social reformers. (I devoted an entire book, *Healing Pluto Problems*, to these valiant souls.)

Outer-Planet People: Commonly encountered in astrology and New Age circles, but seldom in the teller's cage at the bank, these individuals are what I call Outer-Planet People, or OPPs. In their charts, two or more of the outer planets—Uranus, Neptune, and Pluto—are heavily emphasized. There are doubtless subraces of OPPs—the Uranus-Neptune type, the Pluto-Uranus type, the Pluto-Neptune type. However, they share the distinction of not being "of this world" and of feeling set apart and alienated from earthlings. Many would characterize themselves as Starseed. (If you don't know what Starseed are, there is a strong chance that either you aren't an OPP, or you are in denial about your origins.)

OPPs typically do not come into their own until the midlife cycle hits, when they are empowered by double doses of outer-planet energies. (In the late 30s to mid-40s, transiting Neptune squares natal Neptune, Uranus opposes natal Uranus, and Pluto squares natal Pluto.) At that time, they, with others of their generation, gather the courage to fully express the outer planets and to remember their incarnational purposes. With all the outer planets in universal signs for the next several decades, we desperately need their help for Earth to survive and for all of us to shift to a global/galactic culture.

How Signs and Houses Modify Keynote Planets

As you have begun to see, the planet is stronger than the sign. A Sun conjunct Pluto in Libra is no placating pushover; a Saturn conjunct the Moon in Sagittarius is no cockeyed optimist. Yet, the keynote's sign is important, because it forms a kind of overtone. A person whom the table identifies as Venusian can be anything but warm and responsive if Venus is in Capricorn. Instead this may be someone of classic, even elegant style, with cheekbones to die for, although formal and reserved in both social settings and love.

The keynote's sign can deepen your understanding. Suppose Jupiter is your signature planet. This makes you a jovial type, a philosopher and perpetual seeker who wants to uplift, not only yourself, but everyone in your path by sharing what you've learned. The philosophy and studies that appeal to you depend on the sign and major aspects of your Jupiter.

If your Jupiter is in Taurus, you're a homespun philosopher who dishes out great doses of common sense along with old-fashioned principles. With Jupiter in Pisces, you'd be more mystical. You dimly sense, but can't explain, certain truths. You often learn much from meditation or gurus, whether in body or on the astral plane. For some with a badly-aspected Jupiter in Scorpio, the guiding philosophy may be more cynical.

The house position also colors the functioning of the keynote planet. If Mercury is a keynote and falls into the 5th, then creativity, romance, or children are important pursuits. If Mars is a keynote and falls into the 11th, then being a leader in groups or among friends may occupy a great deal of time and energy. Note, however, that one way a planet becomes a keynote is to fall into the Gauquelin sectors. If the planet is in the 9th, but conjunct the Midheaven, then it typifies the career, as well as having some 9th-house coloration. Likewise, if it is in the 6th, but conjunct the Descendant, it affects committed relationships, as well as the workplace.

A Denizen of Neptune and Pluto—Fabio

Let's see how these techniques work. Chart 7 (page 78) shows the horoscope of Fabio, the male model who appears on the cover of countless romance novels. He is the fantasy "hunk" of millions of women worldwide. Few people are born exactly on the hour, so the birth time given here may be rounded-off. Still, I would bet money on that 29 degree Leo Midheaven conjunct the super-Leonine fixed star, Regulus. Does he have a mane or what?

Highlighting the Gauquelin sectors we find Pluto in the 10th house conjunct the Midheaven, while Neptune is in the powerful 10-degree range of the Ascendant, though placed in the 12th house. How well do these two planets describe the public persona of this glamorous sex symbol? Not only are they in the Gauquelin sectors, they are emphasized in other ways. Indeed, we can call Fabio both a Plutonian and a Neptunian.

Pluto rules his Scorpio Ascendant and disposes of Neptune in Scorpio. More importantly, Pluto is the focal planet of a close, mutable T-square. It involves the Moon (his emotional life, the public, and his relationship to women) in Gemini, and Jupiter in its own sign, Sagittarius. Jupiter expands and even exaggerates all it touches. Pluto completes a minor triangle, as it trines Saturn and sextiles Neptune. Moreover, Saturn and Neptune sextile one another. I call this a talent triangle, since there is an easy flow of expression of the three planets involved.

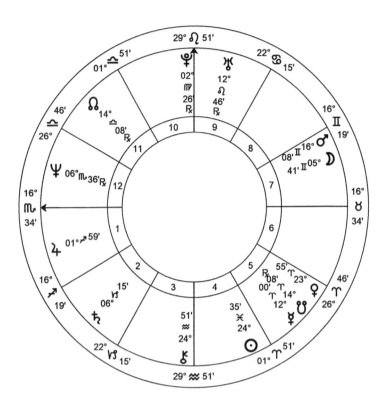

Chart 7. Fabio. Born March 15, 1959, 11:00 P.M. CET, Milan, Italy, 9E11; 45N28. Lois Rodden's Data News, *#46, cites the data from his birth certificate. The chart is in the tropical zodiac, using Placidus houses.*

Besides being in the Gauquelin sector, romantic, fantasy-prone Neptune disposes of Fabio's Pisces Sun and aspects it by a 135-degree angle, called a sesquiquadrate. Neptune forms a close quincunx to his Gemini Moon, so it aspects both the Sun and Moon. (Get out those neon-green pens, because what you might miss otherwise is that Neptune is part of an Eye of God, with Saturn also quincunx the Moon.) Neptune is part of that talent triangle with Pluto and Saturn.

What does it mean that Fabio's keynotes are Pluto and Neptune? Not all Pluto-prominent people are sex symbols, though JFK Jr. has Pluto on the Ascendant. It falls on Fabio's Midheaven, so he became "Fabi-ously" wealthy by turning women on. The public often projects its own needs or its own shadow onto the Plutonian, making them a target of dread or desire—your worst nightmare, your best fantasy.

As the most elevated planet in this chart, Pluto is out there for everyone to see. The equally prominent Neptune, on the other hand, is more difficult to access. It is in the 12th house, in mind-your-own-business Scorpio, and the angles it forms to the Sun and Moon are anything but straightforward.

We can conclude from this that there is much the public doesn't know about Fabio—or perhaps that Fabio doesn't know about himself. He hardly looks like someone with an addiction, as he glows with health. But with that powerful 12th-house Neptune, who knows what his secrets are? Maybe he is a closet mystic, or goes around in disguise doing good deeds. Maybe he is a frog disguised as a prince. Maybe he is an alien disguised as a supermodel. Maybe glamour itself is a prison for him. Poor Fabio.

What Can You Do if You're Not from this Planet?

These all-too-brief descriptions of planetary types may have hit home, and you may be thinking that Earth is not your natural milieu. Each placement has its advantages and disadvantages, and none is entirely negative or positive. Work toward the positive expressions of your planet's energy, consciously choosing not to get stuck in the negative. My books discuss healing tools, like flower remedies, color meditations, affirmations, and crystals, for each planet. As you read other astrologers' books on various planets, additional ideas and approaches will occur to you.

Others of you may still be debating which planets are your keynotes. Chances are, if you're this deeply into astrology, that one of them is either Uranus or Neptune. Astrology is ruled by Uranus, but many astrologers are Neptunian. How can you tell which of the two types people are?

Ask them what day it is today.

If they look at their calendar watches, they're Uranian.

If they look *for* their calendar watches, they're Neptunian.

CHAPTER FIVE

A Guided Tour of the Hard Aspects

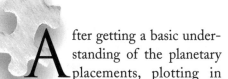

After getting a basic understanding of the planetary placements, plotting in aspects, and finding the signature planets, we turn to individual aspects. We need to grasp the differences between conjunctions, squares, trines, and other combinations. Let's begin with hard angles, for they are the most uncomfortable and, thus, the most likely to produce visible results. Hard aspects—the itches that we scratch—drive us to respond to challenging circumstances and to change them or ourselves. The charts of famous or accomplished people usually have many hard aspects, along with softer ones to help resolve issues suggested by the hard ones.

To understand various aspects, take a single pair of planets as they form a series of angles. Notice how they change as they are conjunct, then square, and then opposite. Begin by considering how friendly and compatible the two planets are in nature. For example, Mercury and Jupiter, or Mercury and Uranus, are all mental in focus, and thus are compatible, and work toward common ends, even in hard aspect. The qualities of Mercury and Saturn, or Mercury and Neptune, are less at ease with one another and have more conflict, even in easy aspects. Let's choose Mercury and Saturn, a challenging yet productive combination, as an example. We will take this pair through a series of aspects in the next several chapters.

You yourself may not have a major Mercury-Saturn aspect. Chances are good that you don't, or you wouldn't be reading something as far out as an astrology text! (Mercury-Uranus, or Mercury-Neptune, would be more likely.) Reading this explanation of aspects, you may wonder, "When do we get to the part about me?"

We may not discuss any of your own aspects—remember, this is not a cookbook. However, you'll absorb a method of combining any pair of planets, so that you won't have to depend on memorized interpretations. To apply this technique to your chart, draw up lists for planets that aspect your Mercury. Follow along on our tour, plugging in concepts for those planets in place of Saturn's.

Step One: Making a Concept List

One way to fathom a planetary pair is to make lists of the qualities, concerns, and functions of both, as we learned to do in chapter three. Look at partial lists for our chosen set:

Mercury	*Saturn*
The influence of siblings;	*Parents, those in authority;*
Communication, language skills;	*Fear, anxiety, inhibition;*
Learning, transfer of ideas;	*Initial limitations, delays;*
Thinking, thought processes;	*Discipline, determination;*

Perceptions, the senses;	*Long-range goals;*
Making connections;	*Barriers overcome by*
The hands, dexterity;	*hard work;*
Humor, mental agility.	*Success, accomplishments;*
	Careers or professions.

Cover up the list for Mercury, and ponder the list for Saturn by itself. As befits the planet most connected with time, there is a chronology—a history that shows how anxieties instilled by parents' demands become the source of limitations and delays. As we persevere, partly because of our parents' expectations, certain goals become meaningful.

Over time (and with overtime!) the very areas in which we initially felt limited and imperfect can lead to our greatest accomplishments. The case of the oyster and the pearl always seemed to me to express the essence of Saturn. Surely the oyster must consider itself afflicted by that grain of sand and probably whines about it a lot. Yet the sand spurs the oyster to create a pearl of great beauty and value.

Next, scan Mercury's list for insights. In listening to clients' histories for many years, it has become clear to me that Mercury, like the 3rd house, describes siblings and their influence on us. Transits to natal Mercury often accompany changes in the lives of our siblings and in our ties with them.

Drawing connections between various meanings of Mercury, I have seen how crucial siblings are in shaping communication and language patterns in youth. As our peers, our siblings, unlike our parents, impart realities of life in the family rec room or backyard realities that adults aren't ready for us to know. "There is no Santa Claus," they whisper, and it turns out to be true. "Wait until Dad's had a few," they counsel, "then hit him up for money for the movies." Their advice works often enough that we tend to listen.

Returning to the lists for Mercury and Saturn, mix and match the items to see what connections you can make. You might intuit that, in many cases, a brother or sister can play into a person's sense of mental inadequacy. Many with this aspect have older siblings who assume too much parental authority and responsibility and thus become overbearing. Perhaps they are even abusive, if these planets combine with difficult signs and other hard aspects.

Continue to link items to see what else you can deduce; let the connections operate on many levels. For instance, certain Mercury-Saturn people are accomplished musicians, often at the piano. This instrument requires strong hands and long fingers, as well as discipline, concentration, and persistence—especially in classical music. A jazz pianist in a successful New York City trio had Mercury conjunct Saturn in Virgo. (One of my mentors, Rod Chase, felt Virgo was connected with jazz, given its precision, intricate detail, and working-class origins.)

Step Two: Developing a Psychological Profile

The next stage in understanding how aspects work is to develop a psychological profile through the lists of functions. These scenarios may not exactly match the experiences of any given individual with a Mercury-Saturn aspect. Instead of having an older sibling who took on too many parental functions, perhaps the native was an older sibling who had to be a family hero and role model to younger siblings.

Life is like fiction in many respects. When you plug in the details, there are thousands of stories, yet when the story line is reduced to bare bones, there are only a few timeless plots. That is to say, certain emotional and behaviorial patterns are common to hard aspects between any pair of planets, including the conjunction, square, opposition, and quincunx. Though the trine is harmonious, it may share a similar plot line with a more supportive cast of characters. People with Saturn in the 3rd house show some qualities of Mercury-Saturn aspects.

Contrasting Saturn's functions with Mercury's, you begin to sense a story. You may suspect the parents in question were critical and perfectionistic as the youngster began first to talk and then to learn other basic skills. The demands of parents and teachers escalate as that first transiting Saturn, square to its natal position, kicks in at age 7, then again at 14 with the opposition. Their perfectionism may make the child feel anxious and inadequate in school and yet also provide motivation to work hard.

To win the approval of authority figures, many of these people attempt skills too advanced for their age, then compare themselves with teachers, rather than peers. Their drive to master these ideas and skills takes them beyond the family's educational background, often past their own comfort level. These aspects are the hallmark of folks who climb the ladder of success because of mental accomplishments, yet remain insecure about their intellect.

Based on the qualities of both these planets, astrologically aware parents whose small offspring have the aspect might be concerned about intellectual deficits or language delays. This is sometimes true—for instance, under heavy performance pressure from parents and other adults, some children with this aspect stutter or become shy about talking. Marlee Matlin, the critically acclaimed deaf actress, has Mercury in Leo quincunx Saturn in Pisces. However, the signature for her deafness is complex, as Mercury was also very slow, retrograde but about to turn direct, and was square Neptune. (According to the *World Almanac*, she was born August 24, 1965, in Morton Grove, IL, but her birth time is unknown.)

A distinguished African-American with a resonant voice and a striking Mercury-Saturn story is actor James Earl Jones. Like Maya Angelou, who has Mercury square Saturn, Jones spent several of his childhood years as a mute, having suffered a trauma. He had apparently told someone that he wished they were dead. When they died shortly thereafter, he concluded that his words had killed them. He was born in Mississippi on January 17, 1931, time unknown. His Mercury is stationary direct at 6 Capricorn, forming a 9-degree conjunction to Saturn at 15 Capricorn. Though this might be considered wide, a stationary planet merits a wider orb. In addition, Saturn disposes of Mercury, and the pair is bridged by the Moon in mid-Capricorn.[1] Even though he is very successful, James still stutters and, to this day, is consumed by terror when he performs.

Even if a child with this aspect appears language-delayed, take heart in the story of Albert Einstein. He didn't speak until he was 2 and was considered retarded when he entered school. He became a renowned physicist who discovered the theory of relativity. Even then, the aspect continued to operate, for his struggle to get his scientific peers to accept that brilliant theory took many years. As chart 8 (page 87) shows, he had Mercury conjunct Saturn in Aries in the 10th house, the only other aspect being a quincunx to Uranus. (He was also a classical pianist.)

Similarly, a young woman in psychotherapy with me was getting her Ph.D. in physics and taught undergraduate sections of the subject, yet was convinced she was stupid. She had a close conjunction of Mercury and Saturn in Aquarius in the 9th house. Like her parents, she compared herself negatively to her older brother, the family hero, who excelled academically before

---

[1]Data from *The Celebrity Who's Who*, by the editors of *Who's Who in America* (New York: World Almanac Books, 1986), p.186.

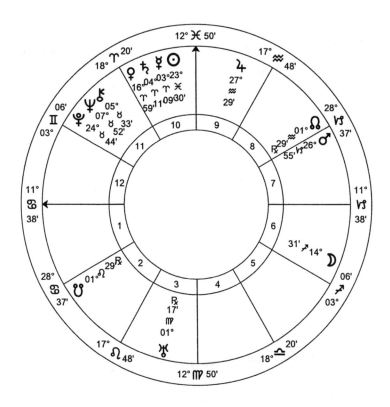

Chart 8. Albert Einstein. Born March 14, 1879, at 11:30 A.M. LMT, Ulm, Germany, 10E00, 48N30. Data noted in Lois Rodden's ASTRO-DATA II as coming from a copy of the birth registration. The chart is in the tropical zodiac, using Placidus houses.

she did. As you might suspect, this type of comparison is frequent with major Mercury-Saturn aspects. Usually, the sibling is five or more years older. The first-grader whose abilities are compared with a sibling in fifth or sixth grade is bound to be far behind. At times, it is not a sibling, but a parent so brilliant that the child feels inadequate to live up to that role model's accomplishments.

I don't wish to minimize the difficulties in this pairing, or to pretend that everyone born with it will earn a Ph.D. After all, thousands of babies were born on the same day as my client, and some of them may be hearing-impaired or suffer from learning disorders. Some of them may not even have finished high school, but I'd wager the dropout rate was no higher than for any other Mercury aspect. Despite their struggles, they have persistence—and parents who care about education—on their side.

The Conjunction—Shared Viewpoints

In conjunctions, two planets stand together and form an alchemical bond, each affecting the other so that they seldom function separately. This is perhaps the most engrossing Mercury-Saturn aspect, as these individuals can seldom be Mercurial without also being Saturnine. They take mental tasks very seriously and pursue them in a disciplined way. After all, we call a demanding and organized field of study or professional path a "discipline" and a committed student a "disciple." At the same time, these people can be facile at making connections (Mercury) between various types of structures and constructs (Saturn). Thus, many of them are good at developing theories or building things.

The studies that attract these people, those they focus on in adulthood, depend on the sign and house of the conjunction. People with Mercury with Saturn in Scorpio may be fascinated by psychology or the occult. Those with Mercury and Saturn together in the 6th house may enter the health fields. They might do so to live up to the example (or fulfill the vocational dream) of an older sibling.

Combining house and sign, a Mercury-Saturn conjunction in Scorpio in the 6th might become a healthcare provider for the elderly—an occupational therapist, perhaps, working on hands. The person may also develop healing hands or end up as a body worker who releases emotional blocks from tissues. Or, given Scorpio's capacity to delve beneath the surface, this person might be a medical researcher.

Suppose Mercury and Saturn are in Virgo in the 2nd house. This shows financial attitudes and practices, among other things. Hopefully, this is not your mate—or an IRS agent scanning your return—for the combination suggests a nit-picking penny-pincher who insists on knowing where every penny goes. I'd hire this person as my accountant, yet utterly dread those paperwork sessions. This is a worrywart who saves for old age, with a keen eye toward compound interest!

Miserly traits like these arise from family teaching about money—perhaps a working-class background with great fear of financial lack. Maybe the older children had to get jobs to keep food on the table. There's almost certainly a hard luck story here. (In case you worry that Saturn in the 2nd dooms you to poverty, however, that placement appears in the chart of more than one millionaire, including Jackie Onassis.)

Place the duo in Sagittarius in the 5th house, and you get still another picture. Saturn, being serious and even somber in nature, is ill-suited to buoyant, enthusiastic Sagittarius. Nor is it at home in the 5th, which has to do with such fun areas of life as fun itself, creativity, romance, and children.

This is someone who thrives on what I call "serious fun"— hobbies like classical Greek, conventions of Civil War buffs, or compiling fifth-harmonic charts on United States presidents. Here is the family member who tracks down six generations of ancestors, traveling back to the old country to delve into musty old records.

As Saturn represents maturity, and even old age, these people thrive on retirement or the empty nest, when they've finally put the kids through college. Relieved of family duties, they have time to pursue cherished interests and maybe even publish the conclusions gained from long years of study.

What do these three Mercury-Saturn aspects say about the key relationship with a sibling? Which older brother or sister would you want for your own? My least favorite would be the conjunction in Scorpio, for whom sarcasm, manipulation, and even intimidation are characteristic. With this sibling, you'd put up with spiders in your bed covers because the threats about what would happen if you told would be much, much worse. The combination in Virgo suggests a helpful, but oh so critical, sibling who means well in those endless efforts to correct and improve you. The pair in Sagittarius seems more kindly and easy-going, if a bit blunt, no doubt an off-handed and valuable mentor. Still, can you really endure five trays of slides of a trip to Katmandu, *again*?

An Enhanced Concept List

Once you move beyond the conjunction, other aspects involve two signs and houses, so it is worthwhile to modify the list. Write down phrases that describe the sign Mercury is in. Make a second list for Saturn's sign. You will start to get a vivid picture of the aspect. Let's take a partial list of phrases associated with Mercury in Aquarius and contrast it with Saturn in Taurus:

Mercury in Aquarius	**Saturn in Taurus**
Ultramodern ideas;	*Old-fashioned approach;*
Theoretical, abstract;	*Practical, concrete;*
Castles in the air;	*Cast in stone;*
Cutting-edge gadgets;	*Tried-and-true methods;*
Scornful of the past;	*The old ways are best;*
Humanitarian causes;	*Bottom-line businessman;*
Radical rhetoric;	*Ultraconservative;*
Defying authority;	*Playing by the rules;*
Off-beat humor.	*Still tells Dad's jokes.*

You can see how drastically different these two placements are and how they conflict. In synastry between two people—for instance, a child with Mercury in Aquarius and a parent with Saturn in Scorpio—it can be a recipe for trouble, especially in adolescence. However, when that square appears in a natal chart, one individual must integrate both planets, and thus both ways of being. Is it any wonder such a person might become pessimistic, anxious, and even depressed at times?

Lists for all the aspects we'll consider would take an entire book. Constructing such lists yourself, however, can deepen your understanding and bring you to even more profound conclusions than we have room for here. The method also stands you in good stead when dealing with aspects very different from Mercury-Saturn pairs. Suppose you have a square between Uranus in Gemini and Venus in Virgo. List functions and concerns for Uranus and phrases to describe Uranus in Gemini. Then devise a list for Venus, and phrases for Venus in Virgo. Mix and match the two. Before long, you will get glimmerings of a rather peculiar perspective on love.

Squares—Conflict and Miscommunication

With the conjunction, at least, an authority figure's and a child's ways of thinking and communicating match, because the two planets are in the same sign. The Mercury-Saturn square brings more tension about mental pursuits, often with greater anxiety about tests and challenges. When signs are square, a youngster's thinking and communication (Mercury) are at odds with the demands of parents, older siblings, or teachers (Saturn).

I have known any number of people with Mercury-Saturn squares who mispronounce big words habitually, not seeming to hear when the correct pronunciation is modeled. Often climbing above the family's educational level, they fasten onto a word they have only read and never heard used. They then mispronounce it, yearning to be accepted by more educated models with larger vocabularies. To end uncertainty, they become rigid in their mistakes.

To grasp the conflicts that the square represents, contrast the qualities of the two signs. Suppose the square is in mutable signs, between Saturn in Virgo and Mercury in Sagittarius. The parent or teacher—represented by Saturn—demands detailed explanations and precise speech and thought. The child ignores detail, leaps ahead to the broader picture, and exaggerates in a burst of enthusiasm. The elder is critical and pulls the child's ideas apart with devastating accuracy.

Like other Mercury-Saturn aspects, these youngsters grow up doubting their intellectual abilities. With mutable signs, the capacity to correct errors and adapt to new learning settings is greater. The person with Mercury in Sagittarius forever seeks mental growth and searches for answers. The Saturn in Virgo facet of their nature spots the flaws in their own theories and refines them. As Saturn is well grounded in Virgo, practical implications may be explored. The result can be a fine, balanced scholar.

What if the square is in fixed signs, however? Consider a square between Saturn in Scorpio and Mercury in Aquarius, for instance. Mercury is an adaptable planet, yet Saturn can be rigid. Individuals with a square in fixed signs can therefore be stubborn and opinionated. Rebellious Aquarius doesn't take kindly to the controlling behavior of Saturn in Scorpio. Adolescence, the age ruled by Aquarius, sounds like a battle royal in which the teen stubbornly espouses wild ideas and language to shock the increasingly restrictive and punitive elders.

Despite an unwillingness to regurgitate the type of rote learning rewarded by exams, these types can be brilliant, penetrating, and innovative thinkers. In adulthood, they blaze new footpaths on the "road less traveled." (People with major Mercury-Saturn aspects do better as the mind matures, making progress in mental skills through practical experience directed toward goals.)

Squares in cardinal signs are dynamic, compelled to resolve tension through action. Suppose Mercury is in Aries, signifying a mind that is apt to jump to conclusions and act without deliberation. Often politically or socially naive, combative or competitive, these outspoken natives let fire impulsively, heedless of consequences.

These traits aren't likely to charm authority figures. The situation becomes even worse when we add Saturn in Cancer. Here we get the impression of an easily-alarmed parent or older sibling who hovers anxiously, wringing their hands over the latest escapades. Is it really overreacting, however, when Junior rashly tackles the highest diving board at age 7 or borrows big brother's skate board without asking and then needs stitches for the fifth time this year?

As these natives mature (and some of them do), the voice of caution becomes internal. Their Mercury in Aries still hungers to blaze trails and explore new ideas, while their Saturn in Cancer worries over consequences of a particular trend of thought. Action wins out, most likely, but with a glance over the shoulder to ensure safety. The result is a canny risk-taker when it comes to thought and communication, one who knows exactly how far to push the envelope. It only remains to talk the boss—or mate—into going along with those risks.

With both squares and oppositions, there is often a second party who isn't keen on the path the native yearns to take. That second party is chosen as an extension of the inner conflict, a mirror of the tugs and pulls between two distinct parts of the native's psyche. That's a good thing to remember when we are tempted to blame others for the consequences of our own choices—and squares do incline to consequences until we learn their lessons.

Clues to the sources of these inner and outer conflicts can be found in the houses involved in the square. If one of the planets is in the 7th house and the other is in the 10th, there is conflict between the need to focus on a career and external achievement on the one hand, and the need for a close, satisfying partnership, on the other. If one planet is in the 11th and the other is in the 8th, sexual tension may build up in friendships. If one planet is in the 6th and the other is in the 9th, the demands of the workaday world may interfere with getting an education or pursuing scholarly and philosophical interests. The trick with a square, as with most hard aspects, is to make time for both sets of needs, so that neither is neglected enough to cause a problem.

The Opposition—Complementary Element, Conflicting Mode

To return to the harmonious connections between fire and air on one side, and earth and water on the other, the opposition proves a special case. Signs 180 degrees apart are in the same mode—cardinal, fixed, or mutable—but in supportive elements. Thus, despite the usual conflicts of interest between signs in the same mode, opposite signs can support one another, especially with conscious work. Earthy Capricorn opposes watery Cancer; airy Gemini opposes fiery Sagittarius. Contrast this with signs which are square to one another and are also in the same mode, but whose elements are not harmonious. Mountain-goat Capricorn squares firecracker Aries, and rocket-ship Sagittarius squares oceanic Pisces.

The two sets of needs shown by an opposition are different, but complementary. There is reciprocity between what one has and that for which the other strives. They can therefore make a good team. Cancer and Capricorn share a need for security—Capricorn's hard work for success in the outer world enhances Cancer's efforts to make a solid home base. Likewise, a supportive home life makes going out among the corporate sharks more bearable. Despite their strong drive, both signs are traditional and conservative, so they may be compatible.

Oriental astrologers relied on this compatibility between opposite signs in the arranged marriages common in the East before the region became so Westernized. Their matchmakers put together people born six months apart, and who therefore had similar outer-planet placements, as well as inner planets in opposite, but complementary, signs. Marriages founded on these principles proved far more durable than our modern ones.

With oppositions, we often note the presence of the Other, who does what is needed for balance. For comfort and convenience, we may draft people to act out the other pole, so we don't vacillate between two sets of urges to the point of inertia. If we are fortunate and receptive, the Other is someone wiser, who reflects back the consequences of our actions and lends perspective on our conflicting desires. In developing a psychological profile, learn the identity of the Other or Others who fulfill those functions.

Whether the native appreciates or resents the Other's efforts to bring balance depends partly on the two signs, especially whether they are cardinal, fixed, or mutable. Terminally curious Gemini's polarity with perpetual-student Sagittarius is likely to create far less friction than hard-headed Taurus' polarity with let-me-make-you-over Scorpio. The nature of the planets involved also contributes. Since Mercury and Jupiter are pals, the aspects are not so "head-banging" as Mercury and Saturn. A Moon-Venus pair is likely to be softer, more conciliatory than the Moon with Uranus.

Again, the houses involved in an opposition often show who the Other is and what the inner and outer conflict revolves around. If one planet is in the 5th house and the other is in the 11th, both friendship and romance are important to the native, who must take care to give equal attention to friends and lovers—and not to confuse the two. In a 2nd-8th house opposition, care must be taken to keep a good balance between the partner's financial contribution and the native's, or money problems are likely to create dissent.

Teeter-Totter or Tug-of-War?

When not in balance, oppositions signify a tug-of-war between the needs of two signs. If the needs become polarized, we stalemate ourselves in pursuit of two opposite goals. Psychology speaks of the self-defeating habit of doing and undoing, in which we achieve a desired outcome, then cancel it out by doing the reverse. The pattern indicates someone with a number of oppositions and no softer aspects to relieve them.

Opposite signs, nonetheless, have both the capacity and the drive to unite polar opposites. This takes work—and maturity—unless the subject is a wise old soul. We learn balance through experience, finding ways to meet both sets of needs in turn. Often, we have to learn it over and over, especially when a transit, progression, or eclipse conjuncts one end of the opposition and temporarily loads the dice in its favor. In time, we mature and don't need the Other to provide balance as often, and our relationships get better.

Oppositions in fixed signs are often inflexible and stubborn. They can break down into armed camps, "Us" against "Them," and refuse to negotiate. Saturn also indicates aging, so you might guess that anyone with Saturn in a fixed sign can become more rigid in later years, without the distractions of hard work to keep them flexible. Thus Mercury-Saturn oppositions in fixed signs incline people to fixed opinions and perspectives. These types don't change their minds readily, even when presented with incontestable evidence contrary to their beliefs.

Suppose Mercury is in Taurus and Saturn in Scorpio—a combination bound to set new parameters for bullheadedness. My teacher, Richard Idemon, described the Scorpio-Taurus axis as the irresistible force and the immovable object. The combination may make a good life insurance salesman, however, or even an actuary, calculating mortality risks as people age, to the company's profit.

Oppositions on the mutable cross show more give and take, and thus give a better opportunity to achieve balance. On the other hand, these individuals can also be distractible, flipping back and forth between various interests without bringing any-thing to completion. ("On the other hand" is a phrase associat-ed with oppositions.)

Take the example of Mercury in Gemini, Saturn in Sagittarius. As with most oppositions, the two signs have com-plementary traits—here, both have inquiring minds and a hunger for knowledge. The individual with Mercury in Gemini is on a perpetual quest for information, without much discrim-ination. Add Saturn in Sagittarius, however, and the person can be discriminating indeed. They can weigh and balance a variety of classical philosophies with a keen eye toward realism and pragmatism.

With this opposition, you sense a series of mentors, starting with Big Sis and that influential third-grade teacher, but con-tinuing wherever Gemini's grasshopper mind leaps. "This isn't Trivial Pursuit," the mentor cautions. "Stop amassing facts, and look for the big picture." With seasoning and many such men-tors, the perpetual student learns to flow naturally from facts and keen observations to overriding connections and larger issues. In maturity, this individual is likely to cover vast intellec-tual ground and have a rich, diverse, scholarly mind.

Saturn's energy can be frustrating in the cardinal signs, as these are so goal-oriented as to be driven. Cardinal types want to get on with it, carry out the plan, and reap the results. The Saturn part of our nature urges us to be careful, take our time, think it through, do it right, and be alert to the consequences. Thus, there is a push-pull, hot-and-cold, hurry-up-and-wait quality to a Saturn opposition in the cardinal signs. Saturn can act as a brake on the desired forward movement.

Imagine an individual with Mercury in impetuous Aries, Saturn in deliberating Libra. There's a combination prone to high blood pressure! Mercury in Aries leaps to conclusions; Saturn in Libra says, "Let's take time to study this and see what those who are older and wiser have to say." This Mercury dreams up exciting plans and pants to rush out and start them. This Saturn says, "Wait! How will this action affect the others?" Mercury in Aries speaks in the heat of anger; Saturn in Libra frets about the people those hot words might have wounded. We often farm out our oppositions to significant others. To avoid manifesting this internal conflict, someone else—like a long-suffering mate—may take on the thankless task of putting a damper on Aries' bright ideas.

Opposite Signs, Opposite Houses

Part of the tendency toward polarization often seen with oppositions occurs because they involve not only opposite signs, but also opposite houses. While squares are three signs apart, but not necessarily three houses apart, and trines are four signs apart, but not always four houses apart, oppositions are inevitably six signs and six houses away from each other.[2]

If you study the meanings and matters of the houses, opposite houses have an intrinsic connection to each other—a kind of reciprocity. When kept in balance, each supports and complements the other in a way that is not necessarily true of other house pairings. Consider the 4th-10th house polarity, which is similar to the Cancer-Capricorn pair. A secure home base can support the wage earner in going out into an often hostile corporate world; the wage earner's contributions make it possible to maintain a satisfying home life.

To return to an earlier example, suppose that Mercury in Taurus is in the 2nd, while Saturn in Scorpio is in the 8th.

---

[2]These differences come from the ways tables of houses are constructed. Look at your chart. The cusp of the 7th house is the opposite degree and sign from the cusp of the 1st. The same is true of the cusps of the 2nd and 8th, the 3rd and 9th, and so on.

Taurus and the 2nd house are naturally connected, as are Scorpio and the 8th, so the repetition of house and sign functions would make the aspect even stronger.

Mercury in Taurus in the second suggests a real financial whiz, full of bright ideas on how to make money, but doubtlessly also full of ideas on how to spend it. Saturn in Scorpio in the 8th sounds fiscally conservative, even miserly. There may be an inner tug-of-war, with Mercury impelling the native to go on periodic spending sprees, then the Saturn part of the psyche creating sleepless nights worrying about debts and devising stringent budgets. Rather than owning responsibility for solvency, the native may farm out Saturn's role—especially since the 8th house can represent the partner's contribution. The partner is virtually forced into the role of the stingy, miserly ogre who doles out household money in dribs and drabs and ruins all Mercury's fun.

Putting the Method to the Test

Are you ready for a pop quiz? You knew there was going to be an exam, didn't you? After all, we're studying Mercury-Saturn aspects, which represent mental tests and challenges, practical uses of theory, and building on what you know. (Too bad that I didn't pick the pair of Venus and Pluto instead. Imagine the final on that one!)

You should be able to take the method we have been following and use it to master an aspect we haven't yet discussed—the quincunx. You can now do this. It's just a matter of making up lists and mixing and matching them, as before. Quincunxes are five signs, or 150 degrees, apart, so they involve odd couples like Cancer and Aquarius or Aries and Virgo. These types would have trouble sitting comfortably through a dinner party together, much less setting up housekeeping. Yet there they are, entrenched in one psyche.

Suppose a poor, besieged Cancer Sun is having a transit from Uranus in Aquarius. Begin by making up contrasting lists of functions for the Sun and Uranus.

The Sun	*Uranus*
The self-concept;	*Radical new concepts;*
The core of my being;	*New facets of the identity;*
The kind of person I am;	*Breaking away from the past;*
The father's influence;	*Rebelling against authority;*
Self-expression;	*Brilliant breakthroughs;*
Self-preservation;	*Broader social changes;*
The very personal;	*The universal;*
Self-involvement;	*Social action, humanism;*
The ego, egotism.	*Detachment.*

Comparing the lists, you begin to get a picture of what anyone who is having a major Uranus transit to the Sun might be going through. However, we want to consider how all those emotional, sensitive, home-loving, traditional Cancers will be affected by Uranus' passage through its own sign—detached, cerebral, ultramodern, experimental, and even iconoclastic Aquarius, a sign that tends to throw the baby out with the bathwater. It would not occur without its stresses, as you may already imagine. For details of what this might be like, make up lists of phrases for Sun in Cancer and for Uranus in Aquarius.

To analyze an actual quincunx, consider also the two houses involved to see what areas the person is struggling to integrate, since they involve needs that are hard to reconcile in the real world. In a 5th-10th house quincunx, the pressures of career may be interfering with the wish for creative self-expression.

Alternately, a stay-at-home Mom may yearn for a career, feeling blocked from it by responsibilities for her children. In a 12th-7th house quincunx, the need to maintain a close and intimate partnership can be at odds with the need for an almost monastic solitude.

By considering the houses and signs involved, you will perceive, more sharply than a book could ever tell you, what stresses a quincunx represents, whether natally, by transit, or between two individuals. This aspect can be fathomed by thoroughly considering both signs and contrasting them to see how very dissimilar they are. For extra credit on this take-home exam, dissect a quincunx in your own chart, or one you've had by transit. By now, you can do that by applying the techniques in this chapter—concept lists and psychological profiles.

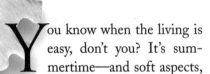

CHAPTER SIX | *Soft Aspects—*
When the Living
is Easy

You know when the living is
easy, don't you? It's summertime—and soft aspects,
like trines and sextiles, have a summertime feel about them.
They're not about working hard; they're about kicking back.
They're not about struggling to put bread on the table; they're
about picking ripe peaches right off the tree. And, yes, they're a
tad lazy, because it's all so easy that you don't really have to make
an effort.

It was no accident that the chapter on hard aspects came
first. I pay more attention to them because they are far more
active in people's lives than the soft aspects. Clients are rarely
desperate for advice about their trines or sextiles, but frequent-
ly ask for help when a transit setting off their hard aspects
brings them to their knees.

We look to hard aspects for insight into the ways people
become their own worst enemies. We look to soft aspects for
support in times of trial—not only external support, like net-

works of friends, but also internal support, like innate talents and abilities. Let's consider how and why these softer angles can help.

Trines—Shared Elements Are the Key

Trines are four signs, or 120 degrees, apart. The signs of the two planets are in a single element—fire to fire, earth to earth, water to water, or air to air. Understanding qualities common to the signs in an element helps you analyze the trine. People whose charts are strong in the air element are good communicators, with a desire for knowledge and information. Fire signs are akin in their vitality, élan, and unquenchable spirit. Earth signs have the traits of practicality, groundedness, and productivity in common. Those with the water element strong share emotional responsiveness, sensitivity, and the capacity to mold themselves to their environment.

One keyword for the trine is "flow." The energies of two planets in trine flow back and forth readily. To observe the energetic pattern, use a protractor to draw a 120-degree angle. Notice that the incline is gentle, but pronounced, like a slide. At 60 degrees, sextiles might also be said to flow, but with only half as much incline, they don't offer the same opportunity to build momentum.

Actually, "momentum" would be another good term for the trine. With little friction or resistance, the movement from one placement to another tends to continue, until there is a conscious effort to stop. That can be either good or bad, depending on how constructive the activity and how crucial it is to know when to stop.

The element involved affects the momentum. Air and water are both free-moving and fluid; fire has pep; earth is more deliberate. (The idea of an earth trine raises the image of an older politician in a committee promising, "With all due speed.") The nature of the planets involved and their degree of compatibility affect the momentum as well. The combined energies of Saturn and Pluto creep at a snail's pace, but Mercury and Jupiter in trine go on and on . . . and on.

The house placements may contribute another, more subtle, layer of elemental harmony to the trine, since trines generally involve houses that are within the same element. For example, both placements may fall into one of the earth houses—the 2nd, 6th, or 10th. In such a case, the easy flow of energy between the two planets bodes well for vocational success. If the trine is between two fire signs and, additionally, falls into two of the earth houses, we get the picture of a go-getter who will go far in some career where "fire in the belly" is required.

Consider instead a trine in water, in which the two planets fall into air houses—Mercury in Scorpio and Saturn in Pisces, for instance. Mercury is in the 3rd house (thought and communication) and Saturn is in the 7th (relatedness). The 7th house is often strong in counselors' charts, so the combination of water's sensitivity to emotions and air's intellect and communication skills might make an able psychotherapist.

Getting Back on the Mercury-Saturn Train

Mercury-Saturn trines are more supportive than hard angles, but are not without difficulty. This individual is still perfectionistic and self-doubting in mental pursuits, yet perseveres and can ultimately become very accomplished. Sometimes the delay occurs because the chosen studies are difficult—classical and scholarly—and require maturity and discipline to master. Still, discipline comes more easily with a trine, for there is less struggle for mastery than with hard aspects.

Suppose we emphasize air, which is Mercury's rightful element. Let's match Mercury in Aquarius with Saturn in Gemini and look at a few phrases:

Mercury in Aquarius	**Saturn in Gemini**
Innovative mind;	*Practical use of ideas;*
Leaps of brilliance;	*Sensible communication;*
Abstract theories;	*Organized presentation;*
Avant garde opinions;	*Adapting the established;*
Quirky sense of humor.	*Dry wit.*

We're looking at a brilliant, yet serious, thinker—not too serious, mind you, to be above cracking a zany joke or pulling your leg to shake you up. The person with Mercury in Aquarius has advanced and even visionary ideas, while the gift of Saturn in Gemini is to popularize those ideas. The result might be a physics professor who writes how-to articles for *Popular Mechanics* or a pop astronomer who inspires us to look at the cosmos. If one must have a Mercury-Saturn aspect, this is a combination to envy.

Not all Mercury-Saturn trines wind up in doctoral programs. Some apply their keen, disciplined minds in other ways, like this second pair in water:

Mercury in Pisces	**Saturn in Scorpio**
Psychic communication;	*Occult research;*
Mystical interests;	*Probing the depths;*
Whimsical ideas;	*Determined efforts;*
Wavering focus;	*Disciplined intentions;*
Creative inspiration;	*Focused achievements;*
Empathic understanding.	*Responsible healer.*

This trine still displays the qualities of Mercury and Saturn—for instance, a good capacity to develop the practical applications of ideas. However, look how different their *modus operandi* is. They support each other in very different ways than the same pair in air signs would do. The focus, persistence, and even the fixity of Saturn in Scorpio is a valuable corrective to dreamy Mercury in Pisces, who can be "spaced-out," drifting, and undisciplined. On the other hand, Mercury in Pisces provides a more spiritual, compassionate perspective on life and humanity than cynical, often pessimistic Saturn in Scorpio. The combination might produce a psychic with substance or a fine artist with perseverance and patience.

We've seen the role of mentor as a possibility for those with Mercury-Saturn aspects. In a trine, the connection and the support are more natural because of similarities between the ways the mentor works and the student learns. With Saturn in Scorpio and Mercury in Pisces, the student can intuit what the teacher is getting at, reading between the lines to grasp Scorpio's unspoken commands. He or she can adapt to this mentor's controlling behavior, if only by evading or giving lip service to the demands, as Mercury in Pisces is prone to do.

For your own learning, try Mercury-Saturn trines in the remaining elements—earth and fire—to see how these elements modify the qualities of this combination. For instance, given fire's energy and zeal, a person with Mercury in Sagittarius and Saturn in Aries might become a marathon runner or even a track star.

Now try this combination in earth signs. Look into the modes of the signs—Capricorn is cardinal, Taurus is fixed, and Virgo is mutable—and make modified concept lists for these combinations. Make sets of lists for Mercury in Capricorn and Saturn in Virgo; then make sets of lists for Mercury in Taurus and Saturn in Virgo.

Which of the two pairs is more capable at business, and which is more academically gifted? For my tax accountant or financial planner, I'd choose Mercury in Taurus trine Saturn in Virgo. For a co-author on a scholarly work, I'd take Mercury in Capricorn trine Saturn in Virgo. At least I wouldn't have to compile the tedious and copious footnotes—nor would I be allowed to!

The Sextile—An Aspect of Ease

Sextiles are facilitators—not movers and shakers, like hard aspects, but part of your support team. They hand you the water bottle and cheer you on as you catch your breath for the last mile of the marathon. They often represent taken-for-granted skills, those that are innate or acquired incidentally, rather than with effort. You may just have a knack. There is a deftness to the angle, just as there is to Mercury itself. It recalls a woman knitting a perfect row of stitches with hardly a glance at the needles as she watches her favorite program. Since sextiles operate while you're barely paying attention, you seldom realize you've done something that others struggle to accomplish. These aspects are handy to have, but are scarcely character building, nor do they produce motivation to change or to accomplish much of anything.

Signs 60 degrees apart involve complementary elements—air with fire, water with earth. Aries, a fire sign, sextiles two of the three air signs, Gemini and Aquarius. Taurus, an earth sign, sextiles two of the three water signs, Cancer and Pisces. Oppositions are another angle in which fire is paired with air (Aries with Libra, Leo with Aquarius, and Sagittarius with Gemini) and earth is paired with water (Taurus with Scorpio, Virgo with Pisces, and Capricorn with Cancer). In the sextile, however, there is no potential conflict of interest, no polarization of the type you see in an opposition.

Instead, sextile signs are cozy together, interacting with the off-handed ease of old high school buddies. They have no need to work at relating, but no particular drama or sizzle to the connection. Leo Suns, Leo Moons, or Leo Risings want to be the life of the party. Pair these placements with a personal planet in Gemini, and you often get natural-born storytellers. Aries people want to lead and, given a sextile to something solid in innovative Aquarius, naturally gravitate to the leading edge. The houses involved identify areas of life where the sextile's handy skills can most readily be deployed.

I often pass over sextiles in chart consultations, especially if time limits and a problem-solving focus are of the essence. I do that because when I describe these abilities to clients, they shrug and say, "Oh, that." That blasé response is so consistent that I have decided the sextile's keyword is, "Oh, that." For the same reason, I use a narrow orb—two or three degrees. Orbs wider than that in a sextile seem ineffectual.

A Last Look at Mercury and Saturn

Let's conclude our discussion of Mercury-Saturn aspects by looking at some sextiles. The person with Mercury in Cancer is preoccupied with domestic concerns, even prone to fret about them. Linking that Mercury with Saturn in Virgo simplifies household tasks by adding effortless order and cleanliness. Here's someone who moves through the home on automatic pilot, eliminating clutter and tidying up without thinking about it, while simultaneously planning tomorrow's supper.

In fact, "effortlessness" is another good word to describe the sextile. Take Mercury in perpetual-student Sagittarius aspecting Saturn in technologically advanced Aquarius. This might be the kind of scholar who'd master computer skills in no time, once it became clear that these tools could make it possible to tap into databases halfway around the world. Consider a hot-dogger with Mercury in go-for-the-gold Capricorn and Saturn in politically-savvy Scorpio. This corporate comer instinctively taps into the psychology of the top executives to present ideas in a way that will appeal to them.

Willie Nelson, whose horoscope we'll scrutinize in the next chapter, has many sextiles, including one between Mercury in Aries and Saturn in Aquarius. Let's see what we can find out about him by doing brief lists of traits for those two planets:

Mercury in Aries	*Saturn in Aquarius*
Forthright communication;	*Stark break with tradition;*
Ever-active mind;	*Quirky but grounded ideas;*
Restless, on the go.	*Spartan and independent.*

We could learn more from this pairing, but you can begin to get the picture of a rebel who tells it like it is, one who wrote many songs, any number of them impromptu, while jamming with pals in the back of a tour bus. The sextile is from the 9th house (travel) to the 6th house (work). The combination suggests someone who can pack sparsely at the drop of a hat and be ready and eager to go on to the next gig. Willie Nelson's song, "On the Road Again," seems an expression of this particular aspect.

Kurt Browning's Sexy Sextiles

A notable with plenty of sextiles is Canada's Kurt Browning, a world champion figure skater many times over, and a charmer both on and off the ice. You may recall him from his TV special, "You Must Remember This." His natal horoscope is shown here as chart 9 (page 111).

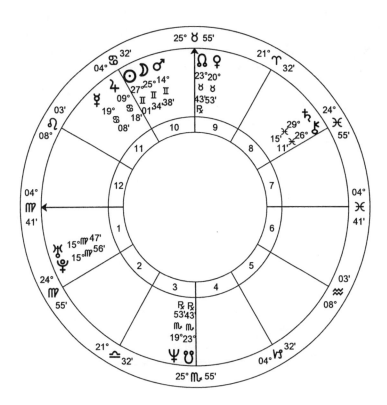

Chart 9. Kurt Browning. Born June 18, 1966, at 10:28 A.M. MST, Rocky Mountain House, Alberta, Canada, 114W55; 52N22. According to Lois Rodden's Data News, #20, *the data was given by his mother to astrologer Jeffrey Simpson. The chart is in the tropical zodiac, using Placidus houses.*

When you draw in the aspects in this chart, the first feature that leaps to the eye is Browning's Venus closely opposite Neptune, with both planets falling into the powerful Gauquelin sectors. Remember that the strongest of these placements is a 9th-house planet conjunct the Midheaven. Venus is here, and the area in the 3rd house within 10 degrees of the IC is also strong, with Neptune there. With this duo of highlighted planets, Kurt is thrust into the public eye because of his attractiveness, charm, and romantic image (Venus), and by his musicality and creativity (Neptune) on ice.

The two highlighted planets are linked by a network of soft aspects that make Kurt a "basket case"—that is, he has a basket formation, a configuration made up of an opposition knit together by an intricate set of sextiles and trines. They are as follows:

> Venus in Taurus opposite Neptune in Scorpio;
> Venus in Taurus sextile Mercury in Cancer;
> Mercury in Cancer sextile Uranus in Virgo;
> Mercury in Cancer sextile Pluto in Virgo;
> Uranus in Virgo sextile Neptune in Scorpio;
> Pluto in Virgo sextile Neptune in Scorpio;
> Venus in Taurus trine Uranus in Virgo;
> Venus in Taurus trine Pluto in Virgo;
> Mercury in Cancer trine Neptune in Scorpio.

This network of well-coordinated, harmonious aspects endows Kurt with incredible coordination on a physical level, not to mention the charisma that has made him a skating sensation. (I'm a fan, if you hadn't guessed.)

How can you interpret all those soft aspects, when they blend together so readily? One at a time! Make lists of traits for any pair of these planets—for instance, the trine between

Uranus in Virgo and Venus in Taurus. First, consider the fit between planet and sign. Venus is at home in Taurus, but Uranus isn't terribly comfortable in Virgo. It's like mixing Aquarius and Virgo together, and yet the placement has produced any number of practical geniuses. Here are just a few possible phrases about that pair of planets:

Uranus in Virgo	*Venus in Taurus*
Brilliant precision;	*Sensuous grace;*
Dazzling detail;	*Mellow warmth;*
Ingenious technique;	*Earthy charm;*
Charismatic craftsmanship.	*Attracts money.*

Next, consider a sextile between Uranus in Virgo and Neptune in Scorpio. This is a so-called generational aspect, because nearly everyone born in the mid-1960s has it. It's more active when one of the two planets is a keynote or in the Gauquelin sectors. Few of that generation use the aspect's potential to the fullest, and some use it in destructive, rather than constructive, ways. (An aspect doesn't care how you use it. If you're on automatic pilot, as you often are with a sextile, it's easy to mosey down the path of least resistance.)

We'll repeat the list for Uranus in Virgo and pair it with phrases for Neptune in Scorpio. Out of many possible expressions of that placement, these seem to apply most:

Uranus in Virgo	*Neptune in Scorpio*
Brilliant precision;	*Artistic intensity;*
Dazzling detail;	*Obsessively creative;*
Ingenious technique;	*Sexual innuendo;*
Charismatic craftsmanship.	*Collective magnetism.*

Have you decided on Kurt's keynote planet? Mercury would be my first choice, given both Sun and Moon in Gemini and many aspects to Mercury. (If you believe Mercury rules Virgo as well as Gemini, you may be even more likely to select Mercury, given the Virgo Ascendant and Pluto and Uranus in that sign.)

Another sextile that may be fruitful to tackle would be the one between Mercury in Cancer and that highlighted Venus in Taurus. Mercury-Venus sextiles are noted for their charm—the gift of blarney is often attributed to them. In Browning's case, Venus is on the Midheaven and Mercury is in the 11th house—the house of friends. Kurt is everybody's friend on the touring circuit, a fact that gets him included in many special events. Mercury-Venus sextiles can convey a touch of grace on the physical level as well. Kurt's lightning footwork is due to sextiles from his Mercury in sensitive Cancer to Venus in sensual Taurus, and to Uranus and Pluto in precision-oriented Virgo.

The Plot Thickens—Kurt's Opposition and Squares

Too many soft aspects and not enough hard ones can result in a talented person with little drive to make something of the gifts those soft aspects promise. One of my long-term clients had a Grand Trine in earth with Sun in Taurus, Moon in Capricorn, and Pluto in Virgo. A Grand Trine is an equilateral triangle with one or more planet in each of the three signs in an element, within the allowable orb for a trine.

This formation is considered lucky and abundantly gifted, though I've known many with Grand Trines who make little use of their potential. My client was one of them. Besides her Grand Trine in fruitful, productive earth, she had many sextiles and oppositions, with no squares to challenge—or motivate—

her. Despite good business potential, she never really focused enough to have a career, or even a steady job.

The Moon-Pluto trine seemed, in this case, to be one major reason, as it signified a mother who was much too willing to shoulder all the responsibility. A chronic enabler, her Mom was always there to bail her out of financial difficulty. Mom would find her a place to stay if she were evicted, or come up with a temporary gig if the power company threatened to turn off the lights.

So, how does Kurt Browning, with his tangle of trines and sextiles, escape being a delightful but indolent ne'er-do-well? He has four crucial squares that generate tension and give him the drive to succeed. The squares are all in the adaptable, but rather scattered, mutable signs. His Geminian "grasshopper" mind stretches between a diversity of interests—skating, commentating, and creating a troupe—and focus can be difficult. Pisces' propensities for dance, romance, and musicality contrast with Virgo's precision/perfection mode and with Gemini's lightness and wit. Still, it is the capacity—and the need—to integrate these qualities, along with his diversity of talents and abilities, that have kept his public fascinated. You never know what he's going to come up with next, you only know you won't be bored.

Mars rules sharp objects, and you can't get much sharper than a skate blade. Mars is involved in two squares—to intensely focused, rather sexy Pluto, and to brilliant, inventive Uranus. These aspects add energy, athletic ability, and competitive drive to the mix. Saturn (discipline, ambition) in Pisces (the feet) squares both the Sun and Moon in Gemini. These Saturn aspects give him a Capricorn-like drive to succeed that you might not expect in a double Gemini.

For additional dynamic tension, look back at that single, prominent, and close opposition—Venus in Taurus on the

Midheaven and Neptune in Scorpio on the IC. Scorpio is sexual, Taurus is sensual. The ladies, in fact, go wild over his often-sizzling routines. Taurus and Scorpio also share a gift for making money, and Kurt is comfortably well-off as a professional skater, working year round in shows.

Where does the tension between the two signs lie? Taurus is mellow, especially with Venus there, and Neptune in Scorpio is intensely emotional. Scorpio, particularly Neptune in that sign, is very private, while Taurus lacks that kind of guardedness or subtlety. Neptune also opposes the Midheaven, increasing the tension between the public and private self. Meanwhile, Venus on the Midheaven thrusts Browning into the public eye as a well-loved celebrity.

How does Kurt resolve the pull between Scorpio and Taurus? Skating, which has to be ruled by Neptune, is a major emotional and physical outlet that allows him to express and integrate his feelings, while remaining externally placid. We can be certain that he also has his defenses and a well-protected private life. The tug-of-war between the two sides is also part of what keeps him growing, ever searching for a perfect expression of the creative tension.

How Would You Like a Soft Life?

Are trines and sextiles sparse in your chart? Do you wish you were one of those people with Grand Trines and other fall-in-your-lap lineups of soft aspects? Don't envy them. As with my client, although much is handed to these individuals and they can be gifted, they may never achieve anything of note, unless there is a balance of hard aspects as well. When you look through collections of notable's charts, like the invaluable *ASTRO-DATA* series by Lois Rodden, you don't see many

Grand Trines. Backbone and grit are more likely with the hard aspects, so hard aspects stimulate people to achieve more.

Of course, it's wonderful to have some trines and sextiles to lend a hand. If you, yourself, are saturated with soft aspects, count your blessings and then get off your duff! Like Jupiter, which promises so much in the way of luck, a soft aspect only works if you work it.

| *Piecing Together the Major Configurations*

When you draw in aspects for charts you are analyzing, do you sometimes notice that they form a triangle or rectangle? If so, perhaps you have spotted a Grand Trine, a T-square, a Yod, or even a Grand Cross—one of the chart features called a major configuration. Major configurations are so called because the dynamics these combinations represent tend to be so major that a person's life is configured around them. Often, one or more of the planets involved becomes a keynote. We'll be learning how to piece together and synthesize the meanings of three of these configurations in this chapter. It is not my purpose here to cover every possible major configuration, but instead to give you the tools to piece them together—the elements and modes, the houses and signs, and the functions lists.

Grand Trines—Too Much of a Good Thing?

When we worked with trines in the last chapter, the keywords were flow, momentum, and ease. That momentum can build to an almost unstoppable pace with a Grand Trine, in which there are one or more planets in each of the three signs in an element, and in which all three of the modes are covered—one or more planets in cardinal signs, one or more in mutable signs, and one or more in fixed signs. For instance, in a fire Grand Trine, there will be at least one planet in Aries, one in Leo, and one in Sagittarius, all within orb of an aspect to one another. The Grand Trine has been called a greased slide, an evocative image. All that ease and harmony can sometimes become too much of a good thing.

In my early days in astrology, I got very excited about one particular generation of people born in the mid-to-late 1940s with a Grand Trine in air—Uranus in Gemini, Neptune in Libra, and any of the personal planets in Aquarius. They seemed brilliant—indeed, they *were* brilliant—but all too often, they talked the talk and didn't bother to walk the walk.

Whatever the element, many with Grand Trines have plenty of ability, yet do nothing in particular with it, to the perennial puzzlement and disappointment of supporters who sense their potential. It can all be too easy for them; too much falls in their lap, with no challenge and no pressure to accomplish anything. They are often enabled in this pattern of doing little with their gifts by family, friends, lovers, and other admirers. They tend not to achieve their promised greatness, unless other factors, like squares and oppositions, set off the formation. Stressful transits and progressions can also bring pressures to bear that call forth their potential.

Although this picture is true of many Grand Trines, the element and the planets involved can modify the picture. Grand Trines in fire can be dynamos, with energy and zest for living that make them perpetual-motion machines. Grand Trines in earth can have excellent business instincts and the gift of fruitfulness. Grand Trines in air, like those discussed above, can have great intellect. Grand Trines in water can shine in the arts or focus on inner development through studies of psychology or spirituality. A Grand Trine with Saturn tends to accomplish more in worldly terms than Grand Trines with Neptune and Uranus. Grand Trines with Mars have more drive to get things done—they just do it with more grace and ease than other Martian types.

The houses involved can also modify the picture significantly, because the signs naturally related to a particular house trio form a subtle overlay. The houses naturally related to earth signs—10, 2, and 6—are career oriented. Thus a Grand Trine in those houses would be more inclined to worldly success. Add the dynamism of fire trines to the productivity of earth houses, and success is highly likely. A Grand Trine in the water houses—4, 8, and 12—may be more oriented to inner life and to introversion. A Grand Trine in the air houses—3, 7, and 11—is strongly oriented toward people, relatedness, and communication. What common thread can you discern in the houses naturally related to the fire signs—the 1st, 5th, and 9th?

A Born Spiritual Leader—The Dalai Lama

The 14th Dalai Lama was born July 6, 1935. See chart 10 (page 122). As seems perfectly fitting for the father of his people and a spiritual leader, he has a Grand Trine of the Sun in Cancer in the 10th house, Jupiter in Scorpio in the 2nd, and Saturn in Pisces in the 6th, but on the cusp of the 5th. The element is water, so he is known for his mastery of the emotions and for his compassion. The focus and discipline that Saturn lends to the combination is shown in his consistently spending four to five hours a day in meditation and spiritual practice. Let's begin by making concept lists for the three planets involved, starting once more with the basics. Again, though these thoughts may

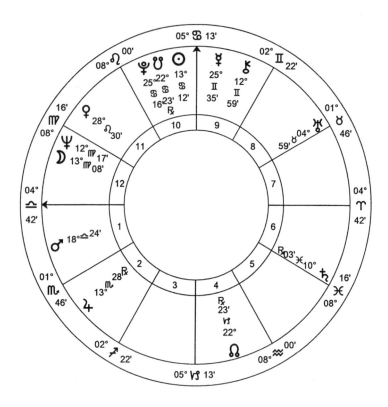

Chart 10. Dalai Lama, XIV. Born July 6, 1935, at 11:45 A.M. ST-7. Takster, Tibet; 101E12; 36N32. As reported in Lois Rodden's Data News, #52, the information was given by him personally to astrologer Marco Columbo. The previously given official time of 6:00 A.M. is considered somewhat suspect, as Eastern holy men are said to be born always at sunrise. (Some sources spell his birthplace Tengster, but his autobiography, My Land and People, *uses Takster.) The chart is drawn in the tropical zodiac, using Placidus houses.*

initially come at random, they can be arranged in a more coherent order in the lists.

Sun's Functions	Qualities of Cancer	Sun in Cancer
Self-knowledge;	Emotions;	Insight into emotions.
Center of his being;	Nurturing others;	Nurturing to the core.
Father image;	His tribe or clan;	Father of his people.
The identity;	Home or homeland;	Identified with Tibet.

Jupiter's Functions	Qualities of Scorpio	Jupiter in Scorpio
Where we seek truth;	Delving deeply;	Study hidden truths.
Philosophy, religion;	Interest in rebirth;	Accept reincarnation.
Knowledge, wisdom;	Fascinated with death;	Book of the Dead.
The higher mind;	Survival beyond death;	Mind as eternal.
Teacher;	Secret knowledge;	Guru or adept.

Saturn's Functions	Qualities of Pisces	Saturn in Pisces
Discipline;	Meditation, chanting;	Spiritual mastery.
Grounded in reality;	The higher planes;	Both Heaven and Earth.
Restrictions, sorrow;	Empathy for others;	Deeply compassionate.
One's authority;	The spiritual realm;	Spiritual authority.
Material success;	Reject the material;	Abdicated office.

Now that we have identified the qualities of the three planets in the Grand Trine, let's begin working with each of the trines in turn.

Sun in Cancer	Jupiter in Scorpio	Effects of the Trine
Insight into emotions;	Mind as eternal;	Mastery of emotions.
Father of his people;	Guru or master;	Natural leader.
Identified with Tibet;	Accept reincarnation;	Reincarnated master.

Jupiter in Scorpio	Saturn in Pisces	Effects of the Trine
Mind as eternal;	Balance Heaven and Earth;	Boundless insight.
Study hidden truth;	Deeply compassionate;	Illuminate suffering.
Guru or adept;	Spiritual mastery;	Master teacher.

Saturn in Pisces	Sun in Cancer	Effects of the Trine
Deeply compassionate;	Nurturing to the core;	Endless love of all.
Balance Heaven and Earth;	Insight into emotions;	Get off the wheel.
Spiritual authority;	Father of his people;	Spiritual head.

Now let's put the three trines together and see how they intermingle:

Sun-Jupiter Trine Trine:	Sun-Saturn Trine	Jupiter-Saturn
Mastery of emotions;	Spiritual mastery;	Get off the wheel.
Nurturing to the core;	Endless love of all;	Illuminate suffering.
Natural leader;	Master teacher;	Spiritual head.

What do the houses add to this picture? Saturn is in the gray area between the 5th and 6th houses, suggesting a beloved servant. The 5th house is the child within, and although the Dalai Lama had heavy responsibilities (Saturn) from early childhood on, a part of his beauty is the loving, childlike quality he retains. His Cancer Sun is in the 10th house conjunct the Midheaven, in the Gauquelin sector, increasing his public impact. Had the Sun been placed in the 12th house and none of these planets in the 10th, we might never have heard of him, or of the plight of Tibet. Jupiter in Scorpio is in the 2nd house, and although he works very hard, he still has never had a job or a business, although his needs have been provided for. The Grand Trine, focused essentially in the earth houses, is part of what brought him to world notice.

If you draw in all the aspects, you note that they form a kite, with the Moon and Neptune conjunct in Virgo in the 12th house, opposite Saturn and forming very close sextiles to two of the other ends of the Grand Trine, the Cancer Sun and Jupiter in Scorpio. Considering his chart as a whole, I would have to say that the Moon and Neptune are his signature planets. The fact that they are in the 12th house adds still more in the way of spiritual insight and power. The duo represents the loss of his homeland and the suffering that has entailed. It also represents the loss of his mother at an early age, when he entered the monastery. We can suspect it was a painful separation for both the boy and his mother. Chiron buffs will note that the Moon-Neptune-Saturn opposition is also part of a tight mutable T-square with Chiron in the 9th.

Note that I focused exclusively on the positive and evolved potentials of these placements, for I fully believe he is one of the more enlightened beings on our planet today. You may wish to compare these positive expressions with the more mixed expressions of Jupiter in Scorpio in chapter three. A somewhat more mundane individual with these planets in these houses, who was still on a higher path, might be the benign head of a green corporation or a responsible investment plan, with the goal—and potential—of making a good living while still responsibly nurturing the Earth. The principle of "Right Livelihood" would be fully cohesive with this Grand Trine. At the lower end of the spectrum, using the negative potentials of these same placements, this could be the adult head of a gang of child thieves, such as we see in some Third World countries.

Willie Nelson and the Finger of Fate

The "Finger of Fate" sounds like the title of one of Willie Nelson's hit records, doesn't it? The song would be a wistful reflection on the strange twists in his life, from years of obscurity in Texas, to getting nowhere in Nashville, to superstardom, to being on the IRS hit list. What I'm referring to here, however, is the Finger of Fate configuration, also known as the Eye of God, or Yod. No other configuration has so many names, or such evocative ones. This, in itself, tells us something about its importance. The Finger of Fate is made up of two planets in sextile, plus a third planet that is 150 degrees from each end of the sextile. See chart 11 for Willie Nelson's Finger of Fate configurations.

Drawing in the aspects, we find, not one, but two interlocking Finger of Fate configurations. In the first Yod, Nelson has Mercury sextile Saturn—which we've already considered—both quincunx Jupiter in Virgo. The second Yod consists of a sextile from Jupiter in Virgo to Moon in Cancer, both quincunx Saturn. The two configurations are interlocked, as both include the quincunx from Saturn to Jupiter. In trying to get a picture of just one of these Yods, we return to the step-by-step keyword list technique.

You can begin to see the poor fit between Saturn in Aquarius and his Cancer Moon by looking at a few of the possible phrases. Placing the lists side by side makes the contrasts stand out starkly. The quincunx is an aspect of incongruity, of qualities that don't fit together at all, and yet are made to do so.

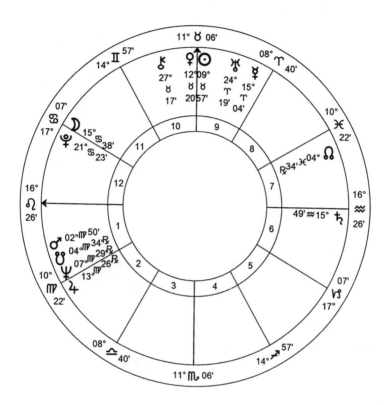

Chart 11. Willie Nelson. As reported in Michel and Françoise Gauquelin's The Gauquelin Book of American Charts, *Willie's birth certificate states that he was born April 30, 1933, 12:30 P.M. CST, Abbott, TX, 97W04; 31N53. The chart is in the tropical zodiac, using Placidus houses.*

Moon in Cancer	**Saturn in Aquarius**
Cherish the past;	*Stark break with tradition.*
Family is everything;	*Just a few old friends.*
Tenderly nurturing;	*Catch you when I can.*
Deeply emotional;	*Coldly detached.*
Just a down-home guy;	*I belong to the world.*

We begin to see that there are unexpected contradictions in Willie's nature. How and where do they play themselves out?

Saturn in Aquarius	**Jupiter in Virgo**
Hard-headed rebel;	*Down-to-earth wisdom.*
Social responsibility;	*Preserve the land.*
Brainy elite;	*Just plain folks.*
Stark break with tradition;	*I believe in what works.*

Quincunxes occur in signs that don't match, yet are forced to work together. The tension of this forced coexistence can sometimes result in leaps of uniqueness or genius. For instance, in Willie's case, Saturn in Aquarius's sense of social responsibility and Jupiter in Virgo's urge to nurture the land brought him to make a wonderful contribution through his annual Farm Aid campaigns. Part of what creates the oft-times brilliant solutions to the Yod's tensions is the sextile between two of the planets, in this case Moon in Cancer and Jupiter in Virgo.

Moon in Cancer	**Jupiter in Virgo**
Cherish the past;	*Down-to-earth wisdom.*
Family is everything;	*Just plain folks.*
Tenderly nurturing;	*Preserve the land.*
Just a down-home guy;	*I believe in what works.*

Sensitive, Down-Home Guy
or Cold-Hearted Cad?

The answer to the above question is a qualified "yes." At different times, Willie Nelson is probably both. He is a highly complex individual, as his chart reveals. On the one hand, he has sensitive, down-home Moon in Cancer in his 11th house (friends). On the other, he has a highly active, but potentially icy, Saturn in Aquarius closely conjunct the Descendant (his relationships). Saturn isn't the warmest of planets to begin with, but in Aquarius, it can be downright arctic. Both that chilly Saturn and his far warmer Sun and Venus in Taurus are in the high-focus Gauquelin sectors we've discussed before—those areas 10 degrees either side of the Midheaven, Descendant, IC, or Ascendant.

Here, they suggest that this quincunx works, in part, through the Other. Icy Saturn in Aquarius is in the 6th house, but actually less than a degree off the Descendant, while that good-old-boy Cancer Moon is in the 11th. Willie's marital woes (Saturn on the Descendant) are nearly as legendary as the loyal ties he feels to his country music friends (the Cancer Moon). With that pair of planets, you get the impression that his strong friendships probably haven't contributed to his marital bliss. And yet, with that doubtlessly well-earned cold shoulder at home, it's no wonder he "just can't wait to get on the road again."

Nelson's chart is very intricate, with a large number of squares, sextiles, trines, and quincunxes, but no oppositions to give him perspective on the variety of conflicts he faces. There is a minor formation I call a talent triangle, made up of trines and sextiles. His sensitive Cancer Moon sextiles both his sensuous Venus in Taurus and his Jupiter in working-class-hero Virgo. Venus and Jupiter also trine one another.

Maya Angelou—The Caged Bird Sings

To wind up this study of chart interpretation, we should consider one example as a whole, so that you get a sense of how to put together all the pieces we've covered. Just as I was considering how to do that, I saw a televised biography of poet Maya Angelou. Her life was so amazing that I went looking for her chart. It was published in Lois Rodden's *Data News*, #39 (see chart 12, page 131).

My first impression, in listening to her story, was that she must have a Mercury-Saturn aspect. She had been raped at the age of 7 and, when she reported it to her family, the man who had done it was found murdered the next day. She concluded that her words had been so powerful that they could kill, so she became mute. Not surprisingly, she has a square of Mercury and Venus in Pisces (poetry, creativity) in the 8th house (sexuality) to Saturn in Sagittarius on the cusp of the 5th. Again, as we see so often with Mercury-Saturn aspects, a teacher or mentor plays an important role in career development. Her six years of silence were broken at age 13, thanks to a beloved teacher who noted Maya's love of poetry and told her that she must not really love it or she would want to hear the words coming out of her own mouth. It worked, and she has seldom been silent or inconspicuous since!

Make yourself a copy of the chart and follow the steps I go through. First check for planets on the angles, in the Gauquelin sectors. Maya Angelous' chart has Neptune in Leo in the 1st house, just 3 degrees from the Ascendant, plus Mars in Aquarius in the 7th, just 4 degrees from the Descendant. Use a pink marker to highlight these two powerful placements, also noting that they are only 1 degree away from being in exact opposition to each other.

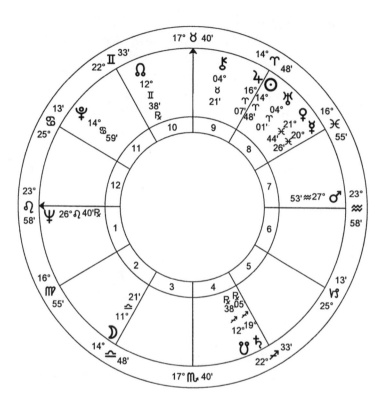

Chart 12. Maya Angelou. Born April 4, 1928, 2:10 P.M., Saint Louis, MO, according to her birth certificate. The chart is in the tropical zodiac, using Placidus houses.

Next, check which houses are active and which are empty. For this purpose, I only count the ten major bodies in the solar system. Her energy is widely dispersed, rather than concentrated, in that there are planets in seven of the twelve houses. This shows her to be a person of diverse interests who tries to develop herself in a range of important areas of life, but who may be capable of spreading herself too thin. Take particular note of the house that is the most occupied, for that is bound to be an important concentration of energy and effort. In this case, the 8th house has four planets, including three personal ones—the Sun, Mercury, and Venus. The Sun's house, as we've seen, is one of the modifiers of the Sun's meaning, so there is a hint of Scorpio about her Sun.

Next, draw in all the aspects. She has a very tight T-square of the Sun and Jupiter in Aries, opposing the Moon in Libra, and both squared by Pluto in Cancer. Given the fact that Pluto aspects her Sun, Moon, and Midheaven, and the fact that she has four planets in the 8th house, Pluto would have to be one of her signature planets. Neptune may be the other, since it is on the Ascendant, and she has two important planets in Pisces. Continue to scan the chart. Do you think she has a Grand Trine in fire? The aspects to Neptune are wide, but the aspects to the Ascendant are closer, and all the fire signs are covered. Certainly, her dynamism, charisma, and energy are what you might expect from a Grand Trine in fire.

By now, you should be able to put the T-square together on your own. Make concept lists for Sun in Aries, Jupiter in Aries, Moon in Libra, and Pluto in Cancer. As you work with the meanings of Pluto and the sign Cancer, you will gain some insights into the generation born with that placement, between 1914 and 1938. Recall the vast social changes that had such an impact on their sense of safety and security—World War I, the Great Depression, and the rise of fascist dictatorships leading up to World War II. Once you have a sense of what each planet means separately, put the concept lists together for each pair of planets in aspect—Sun in Aries as it relates to Moon in Libra, Moon in Libra as it relates to Pluto in Cancer, how the Sun in Aries is modified by the conjunction to Jupiter, and so on. When you have considered the impact of all six aspects, begin combining them as we did for the Dalai Lama's Grand Trine. The process is time consuming, I grant you, but doing a few such T-squares will give you an appreciation of what these "itch-driven" natives live with! And when you've finished with that, try a Grand Cross or two!! Note that, in T-squares and Grand Crosses, the planets all fall within the same mode—that is, all in cardinal, all in fixed, or all in mutable. Thus, understanding the tensions between signs in the same mode helps in understanding the dynamics of these configurations.

Looking for Clusters

When you survey a chart, you often find clusters of three or more placements that aspect one another and act in consort. Clusters represent major, recurring patterns in our lives—both good ones and more difficult ones. Each has its own issues, dynamics, drawbacks, and compulsions. You might call them "subpersonalities." They tend to take on an automatic, yet consistent, life of their own, whether that pattern serves the interests of the whole being or not.

One obvious cluster would be a major configuration such as a T-square or Yod. Another might involve a stellium by sign or house. Less obvious might be planets in close aspect that do not form a major configuration, yet that behave as a unit. Several planets on the angles, even when not in aspect with one another, may act as a cluster. A visual survey identifies "suspects," but, until you track down pertinent transits and ask what developed, you can't be sure it's a bona fide cluster. A transit that sets off one placement in the clump will eventually hit them all. Because of this, the dynamics of the group are periodically brought into focus.

Maya Angelou's chart has three identifiable clusters that represent cohesive parts of her being. The first is her T-square, which represents both childhood wounds and her power as an adult. Next is her close Mercury-Venus conjunction in Pisces, squared by Saturn in Sagittarius, a trio that represents her artistic work. The third grouping is Neptune on her Leo Ascendant, closely opposing Mars in Aquarius on her Descendant. Both planets are in the Gauquelin sectors, very near the angles. That combination represents her often-tumultuous relationship history.

Once you've identified functioning clusters, consider whether individual clusters are linked to one another by aspect, so that they work together rather than acting separately. When one cluster is not linked with the others and does not aspect the chart angles, that subpersonality—and the issues it represents— is not well-integrated. It hides in the houses involved, unseen by most who encounter the native. Suppose there is a difficult, but unintegrated, cluster in the 5th house. The person's often-painful struggles with children, creative self-expression, or romance may use up a great deal of energy, yet be virtually invisible to the outside world.

In Maya Angelou's chart, the Ascendant-Descendant-Mars-Neptune cluster is not tied to the other two by major aspect and stands virtually alone. Already in fixed signs, these placements lack supportive trines and sextiles. Thus, there tends to be a minimal learning curve, and this same pattern has persisted through several marriages. More than one of her major relationships developed with men who did not validate or support her life work and whose actions led her off the path.

On the other hand, her Mercury-Venus-Saturn trio is nicely integrated into the T-square of Sun, Jupiter, Pluto, and the Moon. Saturn trines the Sun and Jupiter, while Mercury and Venus trine Pluto. Thus she is able to use her creative writing—and her highly developed spiritual perspective—to alleviate her painful history and even to be empowered by it. Energy flows in the other direction as well—the powerful and famous people she always attracts have great impact on her thinking and writing.

At times, two clusters may appear to contradict each other. They can be so different, that it is almost as though two people inhabit one body. This often occurs in the charts of those who have been badly abused. (Once I published *Healing Pluto Problems*, the Plutonians of the world made their way to my door.) One set of placements might involve difficult Scorpio-Pluto-8th-house combinations, representing the aftermath of abuse or trauma. Another set of placements might be more lighthearted, fiery, and playful, representing the inner child prior to the trauma. As the individual undertakes to heal the abuse, and as the darker side of the personality lifts, the lighter side is able to re-emerge. In the process of analyzing each placement in a chart, you will become more able to interpret the various clusters you notice in the overview.

Concluding the Natal Chart Survey and Moving on to Transits

In these seven chapters, you have learned to do a survey of the natal chart. You've learned to do an overview of the chart as a whole; you've gone on to find out from what planet the individual comes; you've drawn in the single aspects and looked for major configurations and clusters of planets that function together. In the process, you have begun to understand the principles of aspect analysis. What you've learned will stand you in good stead in the final two chapters of this book, for transiting aspects are not substantially different from natal ones, even though they are, by nature, transient experiences.

CHAPTER EIGHT

Understanding Transits— Another Way to Use Aspects

Your work on aspects can pay off when you analyze transits, for transits are simply aspects in motion. The methods for interpreting transits are thus similar to those you've already learned. The key is in the birth chart, as they set off existing behavior patterns. Suppose Neptune crosses natal Saturn. We can't speculate what the aspect will bring until we see how both Saturn and Neptune operate natally.

To mix the transit's action with patterns of the natal planet, go back to concept lists and psychological profiles. We'll do this only briefly, but if you get stuck, return to the step-by-step method of making lists for planets, signs, and houses. First work with the natal planet, then the transiting one. We'll deal with Venus, as it's time we discussed relationships.

As we proceed, you'll notice that we're spinning stories, in a way we didn't when discussing natal aspects. Transits seem to evoke stories, for they create plot twists in the sagas of our lives. Natal planets are like characters in a play, assembled and waiting to go on stage. They've got a history—what's happened up until now—but it takes a transit to bring them to life. The curtain rises as the antagonist enters from the wings, the hero or heroine faces complications, tension mounts, and the show is underway.[1]

Which Transits Are Important?

In preparing a chart, focus on transits from Jupiter outward in the solar system, for the inner planets move too quickly to produce more than day-to-day events. In truth, I don't pay much attention to Jupiter either, except for conjunctions or when it is stationary, forming a major aspect to a natal position. Popular astrology loves to promise you big boons, bonuses, and benefits when Jupiter is in your sign, no doubt to relieve the gloom of predictions about the outer planets.

Much of this is hyperbole that sets readers up for disappointment when they don't hit the lottery or discover a priceless painting at a yard sale. Jupiter transits can bring windfalls, but they come so easily that we squander them. We win $250 on pull tabs over dinner and go home $20 in debt, after picking up the check for everyone at the table.

When you are anticipating a Jupiter transit, don't just sit back and wait for a fortune to fall into your lap. Jupiter only works if you work it. If you handle your Saturn functions well and lay the groundwork for success, Jupiter aspects can bring opportunities if you are prepared to capitalize on them. Still, as we'll see, a transiting outer planet that trines a natal placement can bring more real progress than a weekend fling with Jupiter ever could.

---

[1]Disclaimer: These are just stories, grossly exaggerated for drama's sake, and do not represent any individual, living or dead. Please don't write angry letters if I criticize your Venus or that of your Significant Other. I know you're not like that.

Saturn transits last about eight months, but the outer planets cross a particular degree, direct and retrograde, forming the same aspects for two years or more. During that interval, you are caught up in inner and outer transformation. Sometimes soul searching and hard work on the psyche culminate in an action or event. At other times, an event appears to be initiated by something external. It catalyzes inner work and growth, as you adapt to shifting demands. The repeated passes over a point weave together external and internal change.

As facets of the horoscope are highlighted by transits, we come to know ourselves and our charts better. Life-transforming outer-planet passages force us to confront ourselves. Hopefully, we learn that the difficulty lies, not so much in what the planets are doing to us, as in what we are doing to ourselves. When we accept that, rather than blame our predicaments on others or the stars, transits seem less an external threat than an opportunity to grow.

How Long Does a Transit Last?

Computer printouts aren't much help here, for most only give the dates on which the transit is exact. In practice, there is a long buildup and a long retreat, as the aspect forms several times. Self-aware individuals feel the transit's effects, to a greater or lesser extent, throughout that period. They also sense its effects as much as 3 degrees either side of the aspect. Aptly, for a planet that obliterates boundaries, Neptune drifts in like a fog bank and spreads out over a wider range than that. Rule-breaking Uranus is surprising and unpredictable, yet at least tends to precision in timing.

Nor is a transit over when it seems to be. Suppose your natal planet is at 14 Aquarius. You may have spent two or more years feeling inundated as Uranus crossed that point, direct and retrograde. Now you breathe a sigh of relief because it's gone all the way to 20 Aquarius and you think it will never retrograde back that far. Wrong. When the transiting planet stations at 17 or even 18, you may have what amounts to a relapse. At this point, you get to remember what you learned. Take that stand one more time, and tie up loose ends.

Stationary periods are particularly powerful.[2] The process you've been working on seems to intensify. Inner and outer conflicts come to a head, even if the aspect is several degrees from exact. This phenomenon is true on a global, as well as a personal, level, for news items during a station take on the coloration of that planet. That is, when Pluto is stationary, there will be a spate of intensely Plutonian events, like mass deaths, hostage situations, and revelations of political chicanery.

Developing Concept Lists for Outer-Planet Transits

Concept lists illuminate aspects, but need to be altered here. Transits represent active processes that change long-standing circumstances and patterns. Thus, action words (verbs) should form the core of these phrases. We'll use the progressive form of the verb (e.g., doing, making, or having), to imply a process, rather than a single event.

The phrases in table 7 are not the only possible expressions, by any means (see page 141). However, they show typical processes, distilled to their essence. You may not experience the steps in the order given and you may repeat a step several times, or stall for long periods. By seeking insight and by being will-

---

[2]Following the ephemeris, note that for a week or two before the date on which an outer planet changes direction and for a week or two after, its zodiacal position doesn't change by more than a minute or two. These are the planetary stations, and they occur both when a planet is turning retrograde and when it is turning direct.

Table 7: Processes You May Experience During an Outer-Planet Transit.

DURING A SATURN TRANSIT	DURING A URANUS TRANSIT	DURING A NEPTUNE TRANSIT	DURING A PLUTO TRANSIT
Confronting lack or loss;	Feeling stifled and restless;	Feeling discontent or lost;	Brooding on wrongs;
Taking responsibility;	Questioning the status quo;	Realizing you're stuck;	Delving into causes of
Eliminating deadwood;	Discovering like-minded	Seeking a white	pain;
Getting your act together;	souls;	knight or savior;	Unearthing the suppressed;
Raising the bar;	Experimenting with	Fooling yourself that	Reacting to your
Performing at peak;	possibility;	you've found one;	discoveries;
Waiting for the right time;	Straining at bonds;	Submerging the self	Accepting your part in it;
Reaping what you have	Bursting out of	in the other;	Healing the wounds;
sown.	confinement;	Finding out you've been had;	Reclaiming your power.
	Reinventing the self;	Turning to spirit for peace.	
	Reconfiguring your life.		

ing to grow, you can gain a great deal. Read the individual lists from top to bottom to understand each planet. Then compare them line by line for differences between planets.

It sounds as if all the impetus here comes from within, doesn't it? You may protest, "But when Pluto crossed my Sun, Dad died, and when Uranus squared my Midheaven, I was fired." Many events do seem completely external—corporations downsize, torrential rains cause a mudslide that wipes out your home, and loved ones die or move away.

These exceptions aside, in more events than we care to admit, we play an equal part. What we are unwilling or unable to do for ourselves, we magnetize. Seldom are we fired without good cause, even if the pink slip doesn't give the real reason. The "other woman" doesn't find fertile ground for stealing your mate unless there is already a serious rift. If you've been deceived, remember what con artists say: You can't con an honest man. Consider the ways in which you've deceived yourself or been deceitful about your own less-than-saintly motives.

Even when the cosmos confronts you with situations beyond your control, you can choose how to use that planet's energy. You can upgrade from an undesirable to a more evolved expression. Examine your part in the situation honestly. You can take the high road and grow along the lines these lists suggest. Or you can dig in and stubbornly refuse to change, blaming your troubles on others. If you balk, the cosmos may escalate the pressure and give you several more opportunities to transform before the transit is over.

No Place to Hide—The Transiting Conjunction

Conjunctions constitute a direct hit. At first, you may feel inundated by the inner and outer changes they bring. As much as you may want to, you cannot run, you cannot hide—you've just got to deal with it. Because of this, conjunctions have the greatest power to impact our lives and, at the same time, to provide the greatest impetus to work on undesirable patterns. They also provide unique opportunities to turn innate strengths and gifts into accomplishments. Have you noticed that while an outer planet is in a particular sign, people with that Sun sign come into prominence? Sometimes they're famous, and sometimes they're infamous.

Saturn may pass over the same degree in your chart more than once, at 29-year intervals, but you are unlikely to experience conjunctions from the slower-moving planets for more than one two-year period in a lifetime. Still, two years is plenty of time to adapt to changing conditions and demands. You'll gradually accomplish the inner and outer transformations you want.

The transiting planet's sign and the matters associated with it must also be taken into account, for they undergo massive change during the transit. It would take us too far afield to consider transiting planets' signs in the depth they deserve here, but it can be a fruitful line of inquiry. Sagittarius is associated with law, education, publishing, and foreign travel, and these areas have altered drastically since Pluto entered Sagittarius in 1995.

Those with major placements in Sagittarius will go through profound adjustments as international events irrevocably change the Jupiter-ruled matters dear to their hearts. We have yet to identify all the ways in which Pluto in Sagittarius can operate on a personal, rather than a global, level. We may suspect it will spur people to be more outspoken about grievances—more self-righteous, moralistic, and litigious—than it did when it was in Scorpio. (If you think political correctness is tough, just wait for what comes next!)

Venus determines love—who appeals to us, what we do to attract love, and what we do with it once we find it. Let's consider Venus in Sagittarius, because, at some point in Pluto's long sojourn in that sign, anyone with that Venus will experience a conjunction from Pluto.

What sort of guy has Venus in Sagittarius? Venus shows how we deal with love, and Sagittarius is a mutable fire sign, so we get a sense of hot, but short-lived, affairs. Sagittarius is ruled by Jupiter, the so-called planet of luck. So Venus in Sagittarius gets lucky a lot—ladies love his warmth, exuberance, and hearty humor. Sagittarius loves to travel, and Venus in Sag has a girl in every port. Sagittarius is the bachelor sign, and Venus in Sagittarius goes around whistling, "Baby, baby, don't get hooked on me."

We have a pretty good idea of how this fellow operates, and we can imagine that he's operated that way ever since those first sweaty, panting nights in the back seat in high school. Things are about to change, as Pluto conjuncts his Venus, pretty much continuously over a two-year period. Plutonia Passionflower—more woman than he's ever had to deal with—comes along and knocks him off his feet. He's bewitched. That's the only explanation. And it's true, she's a grand master at mind games.

The poor victim doesn't know what hit him. He, who never intended to marry and give up his precious freedom, is down on his knees pleading. How does it turn out? Does he wed and remain forever faithful? Or does Plutonia give him a taste of his own medicine and move on with another notch on her belt? It's hard to say, but with Pluto in the picture, this Venus will never be the same. He can't go back to old relationship patterns and live with himself—and it couldn't happen to a nicer fellow.

What about gals with Venus in Sagittarius? They may or may not be as distractible in love as the men who have this placement. However, their relationship patterns will also change and deepen during this transit.

Squaring Off for a Fight—The Transiting Square

Contrast this tale with one about Venus in Virgo, a placement Pluto will square some time during its years in Sagittarius. Put aside the question of how Pluto is modified by its placement in Sagittarius. Develop a profile of traits shared by many with Venus in Virgo. From the description of Pluto transits given in table 7 (page 141), what can we say about its aspects to that Venus? A few possibilities appear below, but, to be sure you master the technique, do your own set of lists.

Venus in Virgo Traits	*Transiting Pluto's Actions*
Unsure of attractiveness;	*Brooding on wrongs;*
Discriminating in choices;	*Delving into causes of pain;*
Faithful, mated for life;	*Unearthing the suppressed;*
Sensual within monogamy;	*Reacting to your discoveries;*
Critical of loved ones;	*Accepting your part in it;*
Helpful friend in need;	*Healing the wounds;*
Potentially a doormat.	*Reclaiming your power.*

When you mix and match these two lists, what impression do you get of the transit? Not exactly a cozy pairing, is it? If this is a married person, marital trouble may well erupt during the transit. Many of these people are long-suffering mates who work hard to make a success of marriage. They support their loved one's endeavors, often at the expense of their own needs. They're critical of their nearest and dearest and not reticent about it, but the intent is to better all concerned.

As Pluto inches closer to the exact square, there can be a slow buildup of resentment on both parts. That is, Mr. or Ms. Venus may come to resent being taken advantage of and taken for granted. The loved one may resent the relentless criticism and detest being an unequal partner and the recipient of so much help. After all, this Venus sign sets it up that way. They believe that being loved depends on giving service and therefore may never insist that the other grow up.

Both sides are falling prey to a stifling codependency. As the aspect continues, resentments can reach a critical mass unless both are willing to work on the pattern. If both are afraid to transform, one may resort to some nasty ploy for ending the relationship. Since monogamy is non-negotiable for Venus in Virgo, an affair may do the trick. Maybe someone else comes into the picture, some unfortunate Plutonian who is set up to be the evil interloper. (I say "set up" advisedly, for seldom do such revenge-driven affairs work.) Instead of infidelity, perhaps there is a different sort of betrayal, or the relationship becomes terminally toxic in some other way.

None of this need happen if both parties are willing to transform undesirable ways of relating. Often, Venus has to insist on the change. If the partner won't go for joint counseling, Mr. or Ms. Venus can still use the transit to understand why they stay in such an unrewarding relationship.

Specifics vary, and much depends on house placement. When Venus is in the 4th or 10th house natally, a parent might be a key player. Where the 5th or 8th are involved, this may be a love affair. In the 6th, the action may occur at the workplace, with coworkers or employees. Typically, there is tension between the matters of the two houses, based on changes in the native's life. New demands come into play, forcing an accommodation.

Suppose Venus in Virgo is natally in the 7th house, and transiting Pluto is in the 10th. Perhaps Ms. Venus in Virgo has gone back to work for the first time since she married. Hubby fumes because she no longer has as much time to devote to him and his perfectionistic standards of housekeeping. She feels guilty at first about no longer having time to iron his socks.

Then she starts to experience the satisfaction of earning her own money, rather than having her skinflint mate dole it out. She starts to enjoy having an impact on the world and having her work valued. She even begins to have a sense of power and can't help contrasting that with how subservient she's been in the marriage. By now, things are *verrrry* tense at home. Still, wouldn't you agree that the Pluto transit isn't simply rocking the boat, that it's finally setting things right?

Venus' natal house shows where important relationships typically occur, but it is not the only place where that dynamic is acted out. Those with Venus in Virgo play the friend-in-need anywhere the heart is touched. Therefore, whatever the tie—mate, child, friend, or boss—the dynamics and the crisis can be similar. It may be necessary to grieve, not only current losses, but old ones. As ties that cannot adapt fall by the wayside, there may be a period of loneliness while healthier new ones slowly develop. In that space of solitude, however, is room to contemplate what went wrong and how to do things differently. Given Pluto's laser vision and relentless confrontation with truth, self-examination can improve relationships in many areas of life.

Transiting Oppositions and the Other

We spoke of the tendency of oppositions to operate through the Other. With a transiting opposition, the Other is probably creating problems for the native. Just as in natal oppositions, the Other's opposition to the native's goals and wishes is mostly illusion. The Other plays an assigned role, specifically chosen to accomplish for the native what the native cannot.

Perhaps the native yearns for change in some essential area, but is stuck. Rather than take responsibility for what must be fixed or left behind, he or she stalls and ultimately provokes someone else into doing it. The boss may be provoked into taking disciplinary action, or the mate into making an ultimatum. The person still has to change, but gets to grouse about how terrible the Other is for insisting on it.

The two houses involved are polar opposites, yet complementary. During the transit, the Other is trying to nag the native into some much-needed balance. The natal planet's placement shows an innate urge to focus energy on the matters of that house to the exclusion of developing other possibilities. The transit causes a pull in the opposite direction. Rather than a detraction, however, it's a necessary correction, opening up a new direction that can prove very fulfilling.

Suppose the natal planet is one of several in the 4th house, showing a tendency to huddle at home and hide from the world. The transiting planet is in the previously unoccupied 10th, forming the first of several oppositions to those 4th house planets. The native is yanked, kicking and screaming, into the workplace and coerced into having a career. Over time, the new direction can prove quite gratifying, but don't try to tell that to Fourth-House Freddy right now.

To continue with Venus, let's look at the transit from Neptune that will affect everyone with Venus in Leo at some point during Neptune's stay in Aquarius. With Venus in Leo, the planet of love and affection is in the fixed-fire sign ruled by the Sun. Consider how it might be affected by the transit of Neptune, the ruler of Pisces, through the fixed-air sign of Aquarius. Start by making concept lists for both Venus and the transiting planet. Here are some of my perspectives on the combination:

Venus in Leo Traits	*Transiting Neptune in Aquarius*
All the warmth of the Sun;	*A cold, foggy decade;*
Party on, Garth;	*It's time we saved the world;*
Make me the center of your life;	*I belong to the collective;*
Our love is here to stay;	*Catch you when I can;*
Pride keeps me looking good.	*Addictive disintegration.*

When you mix and match the two lists, the result sounds a bit dire, does it not? When you create a psychological profile for a female Venus in Leo, you get the impression of a grande dame. She's the "hostess with the mostest," accustomed to being the center of her social set, if not of the entire universe. A warm, loyal mate and friend, she signs on for the long run with those she loves. Okay, she's demanding, and even vain, but she has a heart as big as a house and would give you the Coco Chanel right off her back. (If it's a man, it may be barbecue aprons and the Rolex right off his wrist, but the picture is essentially the same.)

Under Neptune's hazy influence, Madame wearies of loved ones who've become tedious, and thus she's susceptible to glamour, in all its guises. She meets a dyed-in-the-wool Neptunian type—recall our discussion in chapter four—though where she meets this person depends on the houses involved. She decides this is the mate/friend/protégé—whatever—of her dreams, and is totally enamored.

After the honeymoon phase of this enchanting new connection, she wakes up to find that this dream man is in reality her worst nightmare. Rather than receiving the adulation she craves, she's ignored or even rejected. Rather than finding the attentive escort she expects, she gets stood up repeatedly, with the flimsiest of excuses. That wonderfully sensitive, spiritual poet/artist/victim/guru who looked so ready to be saved turns out to have rather sleazy character flaws and pays no more than lip service to reform. If that weren't humiliating enough, now her consort/protégé/child is behaving scandalously. The *shame!*

I don't mean to make fun of such a delightful personage, for despite all Leo's emoting, the pain is real. I'm using my imagination to spin a likely story, but this is only one of many possible scenarios. Being loyal to a fault, the thoroughly disillusioned Venus in Leo may stand by loved ones who are floundering, even though they've become disappointing.

Coping with the loved one's current difficulties or problem behavior, Venus in Leo grows, no longer remaining as self-concerned and demanding. Rather than insist on being the center of the loved one's existence, this person may learn to put aside personal agendas for the good of all. It would be marvelous if Venus in Leo effortlessly evolved in that direction. For many of these hedonistic people, however, suffering may, in fact, provide the necessary impetus. While the end result may be extremely positive, the path to getting there could be painful. I am reminded of the old joke about how the truth will set you free— but first, it will make you miserable.

Neptune in Aquarius, of course, has its higher side, involving our sacred connection to the collective. If heartache ensues, the transit may still teach compassion and help Mme. Venus move past possessive, personal love. At the level of the chakras, Leo is heart-centered. Neptune—especially in Aquarius—is related to the thymus center just above it, which is more detached and concerned with universal love. On an energetic level, then, this potentially difficult transit may jet-propel our subject into the Aquarian Age.

Transiting Trines—Reaping the Harvest

Hard aspects by transiting planets to Venus sound heavy. Let's contrast them with soft ones, beginning with a trine from Venus in Gemini to Uranus in Aquarius. This pair doubly emphasizes the air element, since it involves two signs and two planets with airy qualities. Venus is in a mutable air sign ruled by Mercury, and Uranus is in its own sign, Aquarius, a fixed air sign.

Take time to list the possible traits of Venus in Gemini, then mix them with the actions of transiting Uranus to see what impact the transit could have. Below are some possibilities:

Venus in Gemini Traits	*Transiting Uranus' Patterns*
Changeable in relationships;	*Feeling stifled and restless;*
Likes variety in people;	*Questioning the status quo;*
Outgoing and curious;	*Discovering like-minded souls;*
Enjoys intelligent people;	*Experimenting with possibility;*
Loves to communicate;	*Straining at bonds;*
Has the gift of blarney;	*Bursting out of confinement;*
Warmly expressive;	*Reinventing the self;*
Hates emotional scenes.	*Reconfiguring your life.*

This combination sounds like a party, even without factoring in Uranus' current sign, Aquarius. Being in its own sign makes Uranus more Aquarian and the trine more airborne. Venus in Gemini and Uranus in Aquarius are made for each other. The one-and-a-half to two-year transit should be a heady, almost halcyon time that Venus in Gemini will remember fondly.

Interesting new people—eccentric, but brainy and charismatic Uranians—pop up continually with exciting ideas and activities. Expect all-night conversations with newly-encountered kindred spirits, perhaps on the Internet. Never mind that many of these companions disappear as quickly as they came—Venus in Gemini doesn't care all that much about permanence. The important thing is the stimulating ideas they bring.

The elements play a key part in the flowing action of the transiting trine. An earth trine can be a fruitful reaping of the material rewards of the earth signs' good business sense and productivity. Water trines can bring new depths of insight, understanding, and compassion. Fire trines can refuel and reignite the native's once-boundless energy, which may have lagged from long years of effort.

House positions add more layers of meaning and show the areas of life where opportunities are most likely to manifest. Often, we reap rewards of long-standing work in a seemingly effortless way, as all the pieces finally fall into place. Suppose that the trine is between Venus in Gemini in the 3rd and transiting Uranus in the 7th. This adds still another set of air-like qualities, for these are air houses. There is an even greater capacity to attract new and exciting people and to learn stimulating new ideas through the exchange. If the pair were in the earth houses instead—the 2nd and the 6th, for instance—then new contacts and connections could pay off handsomely in business.

Transiting Sextiles—Lucky Contacts

Discussing the sextile, we noted that it was an angle of off-handed fluency, conveying taken-for-granted skills, too easy to be dynamic. Much the same is true of sextiles from transiting planets to natal ones. There's a burst of support, a run of luck perhaps, but no real motivation to change or produce anything lasting. Often, however, one transiting planet sextiles a natal planet, while another forms a hard angle to it. In such cases, the sextile helps work through the demands of the harder aspect. You're asked to make a difficult transition, but you have support for it.

Let's mix in some ways that transiting Uranus may express itself in Aquarius. (For your own learning, make concept lists for Uranus and Aquarius, then blend them.) Suppose Uranus forms a series of sextiles to Venus in Aries, a cardinal fire sign.

Venus in Aries Traits	*Transiting Uranus in Aquarius*
Active approach to connecting;	*Instant links with strangers;*
Above-board about affection;	*We're all brothers anyway;*
Impatient with subtlety;	*Tell it like it is;*
Takes the initiative in sex;	*Shattering conventions;*
Loves the chase, bores easily.	*Constant flow of new people.*

It sounds like another party—not to mention a consummate argument for safe sex. I don't mean to imply that Venus in Aries or Sagittarius can't be faithful. Many of them are, especially when the Sun and other important placements are next door in the steadfast earth signs. Let's suppose the Venus in question is footloose and fancy free.

The mixture of conquering, gung-ho Aries and friendly, unconventional Aquarius lends a capacity to come on strong and make instant contact. During this transit, Mr. or Ms. Venus is *hot*, with a new-found (but, alas, transient) charisma. Experimenting with a kaleidoscope of styles and social behaviors, the individual develops a new image and a sense of magnetism. Is this just singles-bar heaven, or will it result in a love that lasts? Neither Uranus nor Venus in Aries commits readily. Only start planning a wedding if Venus, the Descendant, or planets in relationship houses also receive favorable aspects.

The Transiting Inconjunct—You've Got to Feel It

To close our study of transits, let's briefly consider the inconjunct. The stresses involved in this process of trying to reconcile the irreconcilable are considerable, but often ignored in the belief that this is a minor aspect. The individual is forced to stretch, to take in new qualities that are not at all related to past experience. As with natal inconjuncts, we can only fathom this aspect by considering the pair of signs involved.

Since the outer planets move so slowly, there was a long period when Pluto was in Scorpio and Uranus and Neptune in Capricorn. Both formed quincunxes to placements in Gemini, so that sign was affected by an Eye of God. That long-range process challenged Geminis to grow beyond the glib, superficial brightness that can be characteristic of this sign. They were required to develop more emotional depth and insight (Scorpio), as well as the tough-minded self-discipline to pursue longer-range goals (Capricorn).

Now Cancer is caught in the same pincer movement, with inconjuncts from Sagittarius and Aquarius. People with important Cancer placements are often home-and-family types whom you can't make leave home on vacation, except perhaps for a family reunion. Many are traditionalists, married to the past—for better or worse. All the matters related to the Moon discussed in chapter two are important to them.

Sagittarius and Aquarius are their least compatible signs, for neither hesitates to tell it like it is, in an unsentimental, even insensitive, fashion. For more insight into the tensions between these signs, make concept lists. Cancers' core qualities are under siege, but they will certainly learn more detachment and objectivity. They will also be challenged to let go, lest the crab lose a claw or two.

Pluto in Sagittarius will also quincunx placements in Taurus along the way. The combination asks these folks to pull up some of that Taurean taproot and develop more of Sagittarius' tumbling-tumbleweed qualities. Uranus and Neptune in Aquarius will quincunx placements in Virgo. These natives will be asked to look beyond petty details and fault-finding to develop a universal compassion and creative solutions for mankind's ills.

Rosie O'Donnell's Success Story—Luck of the Irish, or Just Plain Hard Work?

We've come up with such tidy concept lists for the aspects that it's almost a shame to interject a little reality into our considerations. The trouble is that the outer planets have been traveling in tandem. If you get a transit from one, you nearly always get a transit from another to the same part of your chart. Furthermore, when more than one natal placement falls in the same numerical range, each gets more than one transit at a time. Thus, the total picture is complex, and you have to juggle several transits. Begin by considering each transit separately, then step back and see how they all add up.

Consider a recent example of a life vastly complicated—and enriched—by an intricate set of transits to the Sun and Moon. Rosie O'Donnell was born at the Vernal Equinox. Accordingly, her Sun is at 0 degrees of Aries, a degree that epitomizes that sign's vitality and exuberance, but also its naiveté and continual self-referencing (see chart 13, page 157). Under the influence of several major transits to her Sun, she catapulted into wild success through the forum of her talk show in 1996. That spectacular first year, her book, *Kids are Punny*, became number one on the bestseller list, she hosted glamorous award shows, and she won a Daytime Emmy on May 21, 1997.

Chart 13 is a purely speculative natal chart for Rosie, based on 12:00 noon, because her birth time is unknown at this writing. Printed around the outside wheel are transits for the date her talk show first aired, at 10:00 A.M. on June 10, 1996, in New York City.

In speculating on Rosie's birth time, I chose 12:00 P.M. because the resulting wheel seemed to suit her personality and life circumstances. Cancer Rising makes sense, given her love of children, the close ties with her large, Irish-Catholic family, her struggle with weight, and the impact of her mother's death during her childhood.

House positions for transits also work well in terms of recent events. If the speculative chart is anywhere near right, Saturn had been climbing from the bottom to the top of her chart over a 14-year hemicycle. At age 35, she had been performing in comedy clubs since about age 17, and the timing was right to reap the rewards of her hard work. (Even if the time proves wrong, a noontime chart is no less valid than the usual sunrise chart for an unknown birth time.)

Saturn in early Aries had been crossing her Sun during the months the show was in development. Saturn transits to the Sun, especially conjunctions, challenge people to produce and to live up to their capabilities. This demand can be daunting at first, as they struggle with self-esteem and worthiness issues. When they meet the challenge, the result is more self-worth and confidence to tackle even more challenges as the approximately eight-month aspect continues. Saturn also represents managerial abilities, and Rosie takes a very hands-on, in-charge approach to the show.

While Saturn formed these challenging aspects to Rosie's Sun, two outer planets were forming easy aspects. Pluto in Sagittarius had been trining her Sun, while Uranus in Aquarius sextiled it. It was precisely Rosie's solar qualities that enchanted her public—the fresh, vivacious, unpolished, yet unabashedly narcissistic, character of an Aries Sun. Some of those transits had been in process before the show went on the air, but there were several months of testing, planning, and rehearsal.

Jupiter was also in early Aquarius during part of that period, so she had some lucky breaks. Unlike the action of Jupiter, the luck you get under outer-planet transits is "luck" you work hard to earn and which last longer than Jupiter's windfalls.

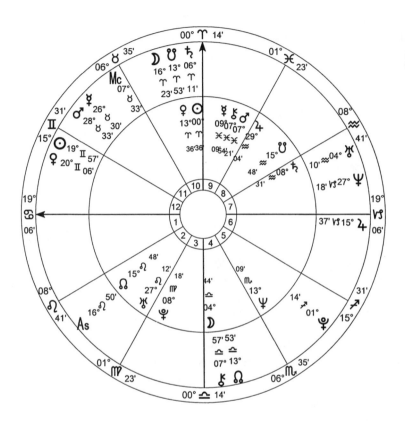

Chart 13. Rosie O'Donnell (with a speculative birth time of noon). As she announced on her television program, she was born on March 21, 1962, Hicksville, Long Island, NY. In the outer ring are transits for the date and time her talk show began: June 10, 1996, at 10:00 A.M. EDT in New York City. The chart is in the tropical zodiac, using Placidus houses.

Those aspects represent the fruition of years of hard work on herself and her craft as a comic and actress.

In the same time frame, since she was born at the Aries-Libra Full Moon, Saturn also opposed her Moon, while Uranus trined it and Pluto sextiled it. A Saturn-Moon aspect can manifest in taking on responsibility for a child and buying a home, as Rosie did. After adopting a child, she decided to leave the comedy and movie circuits and start the talk show, so she would be home for him consistently.

She talks readily about her therapy, and Pluto can represent therapy and healing. Under these aspects to her Moon, her work to develop insight and heal the loss of her mother gave her strength to meet a multitude of new challenges. As a single woman, motherhood was also the fulfillment of many years of longing for a family of her own.

And Much, Much More

Rosie's life gives us a taste of what it's like to juggle several aspects at once, a topic we'll pursue in the next chapter. There is much more to be gained from looking at individual and multiple transits than we've seen so far. Transits have fascinated me for thirty years, and I'll share more about what I've learned about putting the whole picture together. You may wonder why we haven't discussed progressions. Many fine astrologers get as much from analyzing them as from transits. However, transits are such an endless source of psychological insight that I focus exclusively on them, in the quest to go deeper by staying simple.

CHAPTER NINE | *An Overview of Transits—Seeing the Whole Picture*

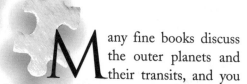

Many fine books discuss the outer planets and their transits, and you can gain a great deal from them. However, even the most comprehensive text can't account for all the factors involved in an individual chart. There are no simple answers and precious few certainties, since each planet has many meanings and levels of expression.

How we reflect the planets at any given time depends on our degree of insight, maturity, and willingness to evolve—something no astrological technique can pinpoint. Moreover, in times of crisis, we often rise to the occasion, overcome our shortcomings, and become heroes. As transits may be harbingers of crisis, it is precisely at the time of a set of major transits that the hero in us may emerge.

Just as you can never step into the same river twice, you can never have the same transit twice. Even the same aspect is never the same. How you handled a Saturn transit seven years ago isn't necessarily how you'll handle it now. Much depends on how hard you've worked in that area of life since the last aspect. We'll discuss these complications and more, moving from the level of individual aspects to an overview, and exploring how to factor in multiple transits.

How Important Is a Particular Transit?

You are likely to experience more than one transit at a time, so how do you decide which is most important? Which should be considered "the governor"? A visual approach can prove helpful here. Plot transits by hand, but not until you have a strong sense of what is important in the birth chart. First draw in natal aspects and identify any major configurations or clusters, so these factors stand out. Look for keynotes, most and least aspected planets, anything in the Gauquelin sectors, and full versus empty natal houses.

As you plot the transits, use a colored pen to show the houses they occupy. These are locations where new processes, situations, and events are developing. House shifts tend to correlate with shifts in focus. However, transits are background influences in the new house until they actually aspect a natal planet, especially by conjunction. My colleague, Gretchen Lawlor, also notes a culminating event in the matters of the previous house just before the permanent shift, when the last aspect is formed.

Use an arrow to show the shift from the prior house to the new one. Planets keep retrograding over a particular point, so it takes time to move entirely out of the prior house. Use a double-headed arrow to indicate both old and new locations until the changeover is complete. (Recall from chapter one that actual house boundaries may be blurred and that cusps vary depending on the system.)

Alongside the house, note the major aspects that each transiting planet forms. Note the dates of exactness as well as degrees and dates of stations, since a stationary planet merits an orb of up to 3 degrees. When more than one major transit becomes exact or is affected by a station in a given month, mark that time as critical.

Step back to see what catches your eye, looking for patterns and stress points that are activated. Is a keynote planet receiving several transits in a short time, or is a major configuration being set off? Is anything affecting the four angles? Are natally empty houses now important because of transits, or are houses that were already full being set off?

The following list shows a variety of ways in which transits become significant.

1. Major transits to the Sun or Moon alter or stress the basic character of the individual. Sometimes, what is evoked is a deeper level of the sign involved—e.g., the Aquarian becomes a more evolved Aquarian.

2. Hard aspects to the MC/IC axis or the Ascendant/Descendant axis alter the foundations of a life; soft aspects to these axes also usher in life-changing events, but in a less jarring way. Natal planets in the Gauquelin sectors need to be factored into the picture—the closer to the angle, the stronger the impact.

3. Hard aspects to planets in a major configuration or a stellium create stress and readjustment in an important, enduring pattern. The process will last from the first such aspect in the series until the final one, bringing the meaning of the whole figure together.

4. Outer planets that travel in hard aspect to one another are an epoch-making combination acting in concert rather than sepa-

rately; natal planets in their path are profoundly impacted (e.g., the 1992-1994 Neptune-Uranus conjunction in Capricorn).

5. Major transits to keynote planets are heavily emphasized. When an outer planet is a keynote, transits by that planet become more important.

6. When an aspect in the birth chart is repeated by transit, the native has an opportunity to learn a new way of using those energies (e.g., Mars is conjunct Neptune natally, and now transiting Neptune squares natal Mars).

7. The more difficult a natal planet is by sign, house, and aspect, the more challenging a hard angle from a transiting planet is likely to be.

8. A natal planet that receives more than one transit at a time, or that has undergone several recent aspects, is likely to become sensitized and thus react more strongly.

9. An unaspected or under-aspected natal planet that receives one or more transits gets a new chance to become more fully integrated into the person's life and awareness.

There is a qualitative difference between hard and soft angles in transits, just as in the birth chart. Hard aspects hit harder and make us confront long-standing issues, so they have more impact. If the planets involved form aspects natally, or if one disposes of the other, the impact will be stronger. A Plutonian having one or more Pluto transits reacts differently from someone whose chart has Pluto in the background. Sometimes they respond better, sometimes worse, depending on how they're using Pluto at this stage of their development. We'll examine these ideas further, but for now, use them as guidelines.

Table 8: A Transit-Tracking Table for 1980–2010.

YEAR	SATURN	CHIRON	URANUS	NEPTUNE	PLUTO
1980	20 ♍–9 ♎	10–18 ♉	21–28 ♏	19–23 ♐	18–24 ♎
1981	3–21 ♎	13–22 ♉	26 ♏–2 ♐	22–25 ♐	21–26 ♎
1982	15 ♎–2 ♏	18–27 ♉	0–6 ♐	24–27 ♐	24–29 ♎
1983	29 ♎–12 ♏	23 ♉–2 ♊	5–10 ♐	26–29 ♐	26 ♎–1 ♏
1984	10–21 ♏	28 ♉–8 ♊	9–13 ♐	29 ♐–1 ♑	29 ♎–3 ♏
1985	21 ♏–1 ♐	3–14 ♊	14–17 ♐	0–3 ♑	1–6 ♏
1986	3–14 ♐	9–21 ♊	18–23 ♐	3–5 ♑	4–9 ♏
1987	14–25 ♐	15–28 ♊	22–27 ♐	5–7 ♑	7–11 ♏
1988	25 ♐–5 ♑	24 ♊–7 ♋	27 ♐–2 ♑	7–9 ♑	9–14 ♏
1989	5–15 ♑	1–16 ♋	1–5 ♑	9–12 ♑	12–17 ♏
1990	15–25 ♑	10–27 ♋	5–9 ♑	12–14 ♑	14–19 ♏
1991	25 ♑–6 ♒	21 ♋–9 ♌	9–13 ♑	13–16 ♑	17–21 ♏
1992	5–18 ♒	3–23 ♌	13–17 ♑	16–18 ♑	20–23 ♏
1993	16 ♒–0 ♓	17 ♌–9 ♍	17–22 ♑	18–20 ♑	22–25 ♏
1994	27 ♒–12 ♓	2–26 ♍	21–26 ♑	20–23 ♑	25–28 ♏
1995	8–24 ♓	20 ♍–13 ♎	25 ♑–0 ♒	22–25 ♑	27 ♏–0 ♐

Table 8: A Transit-Tracking Table for 1980–2010 (cont.).

Year	Saturn	Chiron	Uranus	Neptune	Pluto
1996	19 ♓–7 ♈	7–29 ♎	29 ♑–4 ♒	24–27 ♑	0–3 ♐
1997	1–20 ♈	25 ♎–15 ♏	3–8 ♒	26–29 ♑	2–6 ♐
1998	13 ♈–3 ♉	12–28 ♏	7–12 ♒	28 ♑–0 ♒	5–8 ♐
1999	26 ♈–16 ♉	27 ♏–11 ♐	10–16 ♒	1–4 ♒	7–11 ♐
2000	10 ♉–0 ♊	11–21 ♐	14–20 ♒	3–6 ♒	10–13 ♐
2001	24 ♉–14 ♊	22 ♐–1 ♑	18–25 ♒	5–8 ♒	12–15 ♐
2002	8–28 ♊	2–9 ♑	22–28 ♒	7–10 ♒	14–17 ♐
2003	22 ♊–13 ♋	10–18 ♑	26 ♒–2 ♓	10–13 ♒	17–19 ♐
2004	6–27 ♋	18–26 ♑	0–6 ♓	11–15 ♒	19–22 ♐
2005	20 ♋–11 ♌	25 ♑–3 ♒	3–10 ♓	13–17 ♒	21–24 ♐
2006	4–25 ♌	1–9 ♒	9–14 ♓	15–19 ♒	24–26 ♐
2007	18 ♌–8 ♍	7–15 ♒	11–18 ♓	18–22 ♒	26–28 ♐
2008	1–21 ♍	13–21 ♒	15–22 ♓	20–24 ♒	28 ♐–0 ♑
2009	16 ♍–3 ♎	18–26 ♒	19–26 ♓	22–26 ♒	0–3 ♑
2010	28 ♍–14 ♎	23 ♒–0 ♓	23 ♓–0 ♈	24–28 ♒	2–5 ♑

There are no hard and fast rules for any phase of chart interpretation, since every individual is different. Thankfully, we never know enough to foresee which personality facets may be ready to transform. A seemingly insignificant aspect can be a "sleeper" that turns a life around. It may represent the final piece in a puzzle that someone has grappled with for years. What seems a minor setback to an observer may be the last straw for the subject, who may conclude he or she has had enough and doesn't want to pursue a self-defeating path any longer. On the other hand, even a sextile to one of the more gifted parts our being is a chance to develop and express it more fully.

Table 8 (pages 163-164) shows the range of movement for the outer planets each year from 1980-2010. As these planets move slowly and appear to go retrograde, they may take several years to finish crossing a particular zodiac degree.

Spotting Critical Zones and Eras

To gain an overview of transits, rather than examining them one by one, focus on the chart's critical zones. First, arrange natal planets and angles in numerical, rather than zodiacal, order. A numerical list can help in natal analysis, since aspects and major configurations stand out. In working with transits, it can highlight critical periods. When several planets fall into the same numerical range, this becomes a "hot spot," sensitive to transits or progressions.

The following list shows placements for Maya Angelou, whose birth chart we considered in chapter seven (see chart 12, page 131).

4 ♈ — Uranus (♅)
11 ♎ — Moon (☽)
14 ♈ — Sun (☉)
14 ♋ — Pluto (♇)
16 ♈ — Jupiter (♃)
17 ♉ — Midheaven (MH)
19 ♐ — Saturn (♄)
20 ♓ — Mercury (☿)
21 ♓ — Venus (♀)
23 ♌ — Ascendant (ASC)
26 ♌ — Neptune (♆)
27 ♒ — Mars (♂)

Given the concentration from 11 to 16 degrees of cardinal signs, we discover a tight natal T-square of Sun and Jupiter in Aries, Moon in Libra, and Pluto in Cancer. Any time outer planets pass though the middle of a sign, from roughly 11 to 17 degrees, they aspect a series of important placements, including that T-square and the Midheaven. If you read Maya Angelou's various autobiographies, you will learn that, when that zone was active, her life took one dramatic turn after another. Another sensitive area lies between 23 and 27 degrees of the signs. Uranus stands alone in the list, a clue that its energies stand apart from the flow of the rest of the chart, natally and when affected by transits.

Identify your critical zones, or those of any chart you study. Spot times when that numerical range is set off by a transit. Table 8 gives a condensed version of outer-planet transits from 1980-2010, showing the range each planet covered year by year (see pages 163-164). For instance, in 1980, Saturn covered 19 degrees (from 20 Virgo to 9 Libra), while Uranus covered seven degrees (from 21 to 28 Scorpio) and Pluto covered only five (from 18 to 24 Libra).

Reading down the columns, note that Pluto crossed the degree of 24 Libra repeatedly from 1980 to 1982. Anyone with planets around 24 degrees of a cardinal sign received important aspects from Pluto during much of that period. In Libra, it formed a conjunction. It opposed any planet at 24 Aries and squared planets at 24 Cancer and Capricorn.

Move from your numerical list to the transit list to find your own critical eras. Consult the ephemeris to spot dates when the transits were exact, as well as stationary periods when the impact was powerful. Recall what was going on then, perhaps by reading old journals. You will get some sense of how that range of your chart operated. If it was a disastrous time, don't conclude that future transits will be the same, for the aspects will not be the same and you will not be the same. Those transits taught you lessons, and you have had a chance to mature and work on the expression of those energies, and on yourself, since then.

"The Sky Is Falling!"

Think back to table 7 (page 141) which laid out the typical courses of outer-planet transits. Did any of the lists make you anxious? Maybe Saturn is crossing your Midheaven, and your work habits over the last six months haven't exactly qualified you for Employee of the Year. You fear that the deadwood in your workplace that Saturn is going to clear away is, in fact, you! It may be so—unless you decide to become more responsible and perform at your peak.

Astrology students often worry when looking ahead at outer-planet passages. Transits do herald changes—not *cause*, but *herald*, in the sense of announcing them. Most of us are fearful of major changes, even those which we've yearned for and worked hard to create.

Students seldom, however, get into the panic state I call the "Chicken Little" syndrome. That state is more typical of the novice, who is convinced the sky is falling because of something in an astrology book or magazine.

Chicken Littles write to my Dell Horoscope advice column all the time. Reading that Saturn had gone into Aries, many Aries who only knew their Sun sign became alarmed. They believed they were in for two-and-a-half years of relentless stress. Among them were late-degree Aries who weren't going to hear a peep from Saturn for another two years. (Sun-sign predictions are a leading cause of Saturnophobia.)

These folks knew just enough astrology to freak themselves out. One woman called in hysterics, because she heard Mercury had gone retrograde. Hyperventilating, she gasped that the last time Mercury went retrograde, she got fired, her husband left her for a younger woman, and she was in a car wreck. Now she was being forced to move, and she just couldn't handle Mercury going retrograde again!

You and I know that a transit from an inner planet like Mercury could never accompany that degree of meltdown. Which outer planet would you guess had been active, and to which chart features? My immediate suspicion, which proved correct, was that the woman was experiencing Uranus aspects to all four angles at once.

Magazine articles may create the impression that the sky is falling because they can't be personalized. They can't possibly take into account the level at which you are using both planets. Moreover, just reading about single aspects can't make clear what checks and balances are operating. Rarely is the chart an unmitigated disaster. Often, there are trines or sextiles to the birth planet, either natally or from other current placements.

For example, suppose an executive has had Neptune crossing his Capricorn Sun for a while. He is likely to be burned out on the corporate scene and yearning to chuck it all for some dream he abandoned in youth. Still, he's immobilized and unable to quit his increasingly onerous job because of family responsibilities. Consequently, he's drinking too much to console himself. In his birth chart, however, that besieged Capricorn Sun is trine his Taurus Moon, suggesting a very supportive, down-to-earth wife. It also sextiles his politically savvy Saturn in play-it-close-to-your-chest Scorpio. With these helpful natal aspects, he is able to continue functioning on the job, until he can get clear about his life direction.

It's humbling when the book that frightens a student is one of your own. Any number of people having Pluto transits to the Moon read *Healing Pluto Problems* and became petrified that their mother was going to die. I would point out that they'd had major Pluto angles to the Moon once each decade, sometimes more, and Mom was still around. Even if she were getting on in years, she was at least as likely to retire and move away—another possible expression of that combination.

As these people checked in with me over the course of the dreaded aspect, what inevitably changed was their relationship to both the inner and outer Mom. What determined how much healing occurred was their degree of willingness to tackle issues around that important relationship. Often, changes in the mother's life circumstances and emotional state—for better or worse—created opportunities for the offspring to mature emotionally.

True to the nature of Pluto, if resentment was an issue, working on forgiveness created a powerful healing of lunar concerns on many levels. More than one woman forgave her mother and was suddenly willing to diet. And, yes, some of those mothers did die—moms do that, eventually, even the best and most reliable. In those sad instances, anticipating the aspect and working to resolve long-standing conflicts resulted in better closure.

If a transit anticipated several months in the future highlights a problem placement, start to prepare now. Soul searching about your contribution to the difficulty is a good beginning. The processes suggested in the last chapter are constructive uses of planetary energies. If the affected area is a source of pain, look into healing or counseling methods to stop unproductive patterns. (Several of my books, *Healing Pluto Problems*, *Astrology and Vibrational Healing*, and *Astrology and Spiritual Development*, suggest healing approaches.) Meet the challenge head-on rather than denying or resisting it. Life will change for the better.

An Introvert's View of Transits

Transits operate on many levels, from the most mundane and external to the most inward and emotional. Reacting to external events, extroverts feel imposed on by powerful outside forces—the front office, the IRS, or Neptune. Introverts accept blame for everything, up to and including Mt. Saint Helen's eruption, and compulsively examine their guilt.

Neither view is entirely correct, for we need to consider collective forces and choices, and even the depleted, toxic state of Gaia herself. I lean toward the introvert position, a slant reflected in this discussion. I believe that, as much as we suffer over the painful losses and disruptions that events bring, they are important only in the growth—or backsliding—they catalyze. When we die and rejoin All That Is, that soul development is all we get to keep.

Even a seemingly minor event can stimulate profound growth. Suppose a Saturn transit to the Moon finds us back in our home town for a family reunion. On a mundane level, that trek may result in a five-pound weight gain, secret family recipes for potato salad, and vivid memories of why we detested that cruel Aunt Betty, who teased us so viciously when we were young.

On a more profound level, the event can be a chance to measure our mature selves against the defenseless children we were when those grownups loomed large and overpowering. Among myriad family revelations, we get to see that the once-terrifying Aunt Betty is now reduced to wetting her britches and hobbling about with a walker. By the time the weekend is over, we may even grudgingly feel a little sorry for the old meanie, though her temper hasn't improved one bit.

Being back home changes our experience of the realities of life. We grasp that *we* are now the adults, responsible for ourselves and for those who depend on us—even for that older generation who once nurtured us. Homecoming then represents a poignant rite of passage, well worth the plane fare and those extra workouts at the gym. We fly back saddened, but realistic about the need to provide for our own futures and our children's. The reunion, like most events, has many levels of meaning. What is important is how we use them.

If you are experiencing a Saturn transit to your birth Moon, a family reunion may not be in your future. However, the transit can usher in a parallel process with many of the same effects. In areas of life governed by the Moon, Saturn-related conditions will develop. As situations unfold, we process them, then make changes accordingly. For each action we take, those around us have reactions, and the ties are altered.

"It's More Complicated Than That"

A single transit is generally part of a series, so you need to consider the warp and weave of the whole chart, rather than just one facet. As we learned in chapter seven, planets in a T-square, stellium, or some other cluster, act in consort as well as individually. When an outer planet transits such a line-up, the impact will be different for the first such aspect (we are less prepared and more overwhelmed) than it will be for the mid-series, when the change is well underway. It is different, as well, at the end of the series, when we have adapted (or resisted adapting) and are tying up loose ends.

The dance becomes even more intricate when natal aspects are close. The transiting planet goes direct and retrograde over each point several times. All the planets operate at once and in an ever-shifting way. Pluto and Neptune have traveled in sextile since most of us were born, so Pluto and Neptune impact the same chart positions closely in time.

With several passages over each point, we hopefully upgrade our uses of these energies. People do change during a transit—especially given the gift of astrology's perspective on their lives. A consultation can be a lighthouse in a storm. Given the chart's potential as a transformational tool, do you really want all the answers about how a given aspect will play out? Wouldn't you rather people surprised you with their capacity for growth?

Considering how complex the picture can be, you may wonder how to make sense of it. Use the techniques we have already practiced, one aspect at a time, then step back for a broader picture. The birth chart can be crucial in learning which planets are keynotes and what the meaning of each natal placement may be.

One Man's Pluto is Another Man's Poison

Different people react differently to the same transit. One person undergoing the Pluto crossing of natal Neptune that happens in the late 20s may have a spiritual awakening. Another descends into addiction. One talented writer having a Saturn opposition to Mercury meets the challenge by polishing articles to the hilt and daring to submit them again and again. Under the same aspect, another writer, just as gifted, cringes in fear after one rejection and gives up all hope of a writing career. One hidebound Taurus may react to Uranus' square to her Sun by digging in her heels and refusing to change, until an accident forces change upon her. Another Taurean may react to the same transit by embracing the new, bringing exciting ideas and people into her life.

It is also important to consider whether the planet—either the natal or transiting one—is a keynote. A solar type may react differently to transits to the Sun than someone whose Sun is weaker. For many Sun-prominent folks, ego is a big concern, so an event that deflates the ego can be devastating, at least temporarily. For others, that prominent Sun means the evolution of the self and its expression may be a lifetime effort. The transit can precipitate a reaping of the rewards of all that work. At other points in the life cycle, Sun transits herald the need to rethink who we have become and how to express newly emerging facets of the self.

For one person, a Saturn passage over the Sun may be relatively easy—a time when years of hard work result in a well-deserved promotion. Another, less-disciplined individual's transit may result in a well-deserved *demotion*. Much depends on how people have used Saturn's energies of late.

You can find clues in the birth chart, given the strength and difficulty of the Sun and Saturn. Still, you never know how people originally expressed the two and how they are expressing them now unless you ask. For example, what happened seven years ago, when Saturn last formed a hard aspect to their Sun? Was it a wake-up call that galvanized them into setting higher standards? Did it motivate them to get serious about using their gifts and strengths? Has disciplined hard work toward certain goals been underway for some time?

Another factor may be whether the transiting aspect is already present in the birth chart. A person who has a major Sun-Saturn aspect natally will react differently from someone who does not, or someone who only has a sextile. The individual who has struggled mightily since childhood with this aspect's self-doubt and demanding authority figures has experience coping with such pressures. The person with no natal Saturn-Sun tie has little experience with these challenges and, thus, may be overwhelmed.

How each ultimately rises to the challenge is not something the horoscope reveals. One person with a natal Sun-Saturn aspect may respond with even more determination to achieve mastery and come into their own at last. For other Sun-Saturn natives, the transit may represent one final, crushing defeat that makes them give up in despair. Saturn transits have a way of testing our mettle.

Age can also be important—the same individual may react differently at different times in the life cycle. As books like Gail Sheehy's *Passages* teach us, where we are in our life cycle has much to do with how we respond to new challenges. Hopefully, as we mature and grow, we evolve in our usage of each planet's energy. Thus, a Saturn transit to the Sun at age 21 or 28 can be a very different experience from the same transit at 42 or 57. A 21-year-old woman having such a transit might be finishing college and contemplating—with pride and trepidation—her first real job. A 57-year-old is at the peak of her career, looking back on the climb, yet already looking toward retirement.

"How Am I Doing?"

You may wonder how to assess at what level you are expressing a placement. There are no personality tests for that purpose yet, although it would be perfectly possible to design one, with subscales and scores for each planet. I hope some bright, enterprising astrologer with a Psychology degree will do just that, so we can actually measure how we're doing at any given time. (Though there are times, even after working for thirty years to express it positively, that I'd hate to know my Pluto percentile!) Until such an instrument is available, we just have to estimate the effect.

Go back to the sections in chapter three where we contrasted positive and negative expressions of a natal planet's sign and house (pages 47-64). Do that for the natal placements, to assess how each is being used. Imagine that someone with Venus in Pisces is having a square from Pluto in Sagittarius. Recall our list of expressions of Venus in Pisces:

Venus Functions	*Venus in Pisces +*	*Venus in Pisces –*
Whom or what is loved;	*The highest in all;*	*Drunks, sinners;*
How freely they love;	*Unconditional love;*	*The more it hurts;*
How they express love;	*Sensitive, romantic;*	*Sentimental,*
How they attract love;	*Helping others;*	*maudlin;*
Their sense of beauty;	*Hazy pastels;*	*Abasing themselves;*
Capacity to compromise;	*Empathic perspective;*	*Christ on a cross;*
How harmony is sought.	*Soul accord.*	*Allowing abuse;*
		Giving in too much

Ask your subject—or ask yourself, if this is your chart—questions to determine whether Venus is being used in mainly healthy or self-destructive ways. Use the transit-tracker to spot critical eras when the placement was being set off, and inquire into them.

You need to consider which major aspects the natal planet forms, in order to grasp what patterns are being evoked. Imagine your subject has a natal opposition from Venus in

Pisces to Pluto in Virgo. Analyze that aspect and ask questions about how it currently functions. Maybe it got her into all kinds of trouble early on. However, she's had years of therapy, attending Codependency Anonymous meetings, and reading every self-help book to hit the New York Times Bestseller List. She no longer bites when those tantalizing Plutonians wave the make-me-over-and-I'm-all-yours carrot.

Now the subject is 40-something and, as part of the midlife cycle, Pluto in Sagittarius squares both natal Venus and natal Pluto. All that splendid recovery is bound to be challenged, perhaps bringing on the father of all wounded Plutonians. Still, I'm confident she'll figure him out quickly and avoid trouble. If someone with those placements never gave a moment's thought to why the need to make someone over wasn't a particularly good reason to get involved, I'd be more concerned. Still, even someone who expresses the combination in masochistic ways can use the transit—and the ensuing debacle—to heal.

Given free will and the soul's complexities, you cannot tell how people will respond, even if you have a fair idea of how they've used that placement. You can only find that out by listening. Moreover, you cannot tell during the first passage of the series. People are bound to grow and adapt to new demands in the course of retrograde and direct passages over the same point. At any point, we can choose to take the high road, and we can continue making sane choices, moment by moment, until they feel natural.

Facing the Difficult Potentials of a Transit

Many in our field insist on being terminally positive, refusing to acknowledge that bad things regularly happen to good people. They recite a glowing litany of evolved expressions, neglecting to mention that pain and struggle may be involved in ascending to those lofty places. Clients who then experience the transit as agony blame themselves for not achieving such elevated results. They wind up concluding they are among the metaphysically challenged.

Considering a transit's potentials, a balanced approach may be to include a range of manifestations, from the best to the more difficult. How can you know whether the worst, indeed, may be about to happen? A classical rule is that nothing happens during a transit or progression that is not promised in the birth chart. Scrutinize the birth chart to see whether its placements suggest the kind of situation you are concerned about.

Going back to that Pluto transit to the Moon, what if this is a young child's chart, and you—the mother, grandmother, or uncle—are worried that the child may lose its mother. Check the birth chart to see if it suggests the loss of a mother figure at an early age—not just in one way, but in several. Adopt the classical Rule of Three—if the chart shows something once, it's potential; twice, it's possible; thrice, it's highly likely.

Suppose there is a lovely, untroubled Moon, such as Moon in Taurus trining Jupiter in Virgo. If this is so, the transit may represent another major shift in family life. It may show an ailing grandparent moving in, a new and not entirely welcome sibling on the way, or a temporary time of stress in the life of the child's mother (e.g., grief over the loss of someone she loves).

When a difficult transit sets off an already difficult natal combination, assess whether the person has learned to use those placements well, or whether they are acting out the more negative expressions. Suppose a woman has a Mars-Pluto conjunction in the 7th house natally, suggesting a controlling, aggressive, or even abusive mate. Now, transiting Pluto is beginning a series of squares to that conjunction. Should you worry about this transit? Begin by looking into her history. Ask about the relationship in which she is involved and what happened in other committed relationships. Is she involved now with someone who is abusive or who has a history of abusing women, or has she been involved with such men? Suppose she has never been harmed by a live-in lover or husband, and she, instead, has gone for dynamos who are highly successful. She has obviously not gotten entrenched in a pattern of abuse and is not likely to evoke one now. I'd relax a bit, but if the reverse were true, I'd be extremely concerned and would talk to her about getting help.

The historical perspective can be a powerful preventive tool. In my days as a mentor, an astrologer submitted work done for a consultation with a mountain climber who was preparing for a dangerous climb. His birth chart had a difficult combination of planets on the angles, and transiting Saturn was setting them off. Being a positive person, she assumed that he would succeed in his goal, but she did not consider the possibility of a fall.

Saturn transits tend to recur at seven-year intervals. Noting that Saturn had set off the same difficult group of natal placements seven years earlier, I asked what had happened then. Indeed, he had suffered a terrible fall that required years of recovery. I concluded that the coming Saturn transit would be anything but a good time to tackle a challenging peak. This example shows how important it is to ask pertinent questions about the subject's history, rather than jump to conclusions about what a transit will bring.

While the terminally positive may find this approach a downer, we have a responsibility to present reality checks when people act in ways that are not in their best interest. Warning about the worst, though not in an alarmist fashion, we may help to avert it. Honest confrontation can stimulate people to grow away from negative expressions, given the objectivity the chart can provide. Seek a balanced perspective—neither the most negative expression, nor the terminally positive.

Explore natal patterns being set off by a transit. If a pattern has proved troublesome in the past, it may be an opportunity to master the difficulties, rather than fall, automaton-like, into self-sabotage. Return to the transit tracker to spot times when critical zones were active. This line of inquiry can provide clues to the dynamics of any pattern that is periodically evoked and to how the person is likely to respond.

We've been through a unique period of human history in which more self-help, recovery, and personal growth materials are available than ever before. It's good to know about those materials, so we can recommend them. People's work to become more conscious can alter the nature of any transit. I would never want to be accused of being 100 percent accurate. If I were, I would not be doing my job of waking people up.

"I'm Allergic to Neptune!"

One clue to a transit's effects is the current extent of sensitivity to that planet. Much as people become sensitized to pollens or other allergens, they can become sensitized to a planet. Susceptibility may come though painful natal aspects—perhaps a keynote planet in a difficult sign, with many tough aspects. Sensitization can develop with repeated difficult transits to or from that planet. If the planet is Neptune, for instance, then both transits to natal Neptune and activity from transiting Neptune to key natal placements can increase sensitivity.

Difficult aspects or combinations in the birth chart can become sensitized through a series of transits. This is true now of planets at the end of cardinal signs. Imagine a Venus-Neptune conjunction in the last 5 degrees of Libra. This pair is prone to romantic illusions and codependent relationships with addictive or otherwise disappointing partners. Several times during 1982 and 1983, those degrees of Libra were crossed by a very difficult conjunction of transiting Pluto and Saturn. Many felt that their worlds ended at that time—or at least that certain romantic dreams died excruciating deaths.

In recent years, first Saturn, then Uranus, and then Neptune at the end of Capricorn squared this already-sensitized degree area. This could have seemed virtually the last straw where commitment was concerned. Whatever lessons had not been learned through bitter past disappointments at this point were bound to be confronted and, hopefully, mastered.

Sensitivity can also increase when a single planet forms a series of hard transits to various chart placements over a short period. This can happen when there is a tight T-square, and a transiting planet conjuncts one end, then squares another end, and, finally, opposes the third. This series of aspects repeats several times over two or more years, given retrograde motion.

How does sensitization to an outer planet work? It works in a way similar to what occurs when you become sensitized to pollen. You may even suffer from the same red eyes and runny nose, only, in this instance, from crying. You react more intensely to transits from or to such a planet. Early in the transit, you may be more overwhelmed, with more unfinished issues evoked. You may exhibit more of the traits of that planet than before.

Those who are already strongly Plutonian, or who have had a difficult series of Pluto transits, may react very strongly to even the earliest stages of a new Pluto transit. Old betrayals may obsess them, old grief may be evoked, and they may withdraw or become highly suspicious of others. A Neptune-sensitized person may become even more unfocused, enter into denial, and become unwilling to function in daily tasks. A Saturn-sensitized workaholic may increase perfectionistic demands, work around the clock, and still feel anxious and depressed. Naturally, if you've worked hard on spiritual and personal development over the years, you may react by going into hyperdrive on the positive qualities of the transiting planet, rather than the negative ones.

There are no pat answers about who can become sensitized and when. Until we know enough to develop allergy patch tests for planets, we are stuck with delving into personal history. Discussing aspects of the previous year or two, you come to know when Pluto has been exerting its influence. Growth sometimes comes from repeated prodding that forces you to surrender to the lessons the universe is trying to teach. If you suspect you are becoming sensitized to a planet, get to work on the issues it represents. Consult healers or counselors, get your hands on the latest self-help literature, or go to a support group.

A chart consultation can provide needed insight, even in retrospect. Familiarize yourself with the whole spectrum of expressions of the placements in question, from the most evolved to the most destructive. Each time you find yourself expressing the negative potential, make a conscious choice to move to a higher expression instead. For example, if you are playing the Neptune victim to an alcoholic spouse, try Al-Anon.

Life-Transforming Transits to the Four Angles

The four angles—the Ascendant, Midheaven, Descendant, and IC—really consist of two pairs—the 4th-10th axis and the 1st-7th axis. The Midheaven, or MC, is the same degree as the IC, but in the opposite sign; the Ascendant is the same degree as the Descendant, but in the opposite sign. Thus, when a transit aspects one of the pair, it simultaneously aspects the other. Situations that heat up on one side of the axis affect matters on the other side as well. When Uranus aspects the MC, a job transfer may be in the works; since Uranus simultaneously aspects the IC, the transfer may require a geographic relocation. A planet aspecting the Ascendant will simultaneously aspect the Descendant. As we modify our presentation of self, our most intimate connections adjust accordingly.

When a planet crosses an angle, the process that unfolded in the previous house now impacts the new one. Suppose that, for ten years, a planet was traveling through the 12th house, which, among other things, represents secrets, self-sabotage, and the unconscious. When it finally emerges from the 12th to cross the Ascendant, an important event or a change in the individual's approach to the outside world is likely. Something underground comes to light, and everyone and everything around the person has to adapt. Whether the change is positive or negative depends on whether that planet's energies were deployed in constructive or self-abusive ways while it was in the 12th.

Those who use Pluto's long stay in the 12th house to uncover and heal unconscious fears about power may learn how to use it constructively. When Pluto crosses the Ascendant—and simultaneously opposes the Descendant—they learn to stop giving away their power to their partner and others, sometimes through painful lessons. They then bring out their own capacity to impact the world for the good of all.

What about people who use Pluto's stay in the 12th house to plunge deeper into compulsive, self-destructive behavior? When Pluto crosses the Ascendant, they may possibly experience a life-and-death crisis. Even then, the very intensity of the experience may sober them enough to turn their lives around. This is not something you can predict, for we all have free will and can be redeemed in a moment's illumination.

Suppose a planet that has had a long stay in the 9th house (higher education, the higher mind) crosses the Midheaven into the 10th. Formal or independent studies of previous years are introduced into the workplace and mark a distinct career departure. Third-house transits can also indicate study, though often in intermittent, less formal programs, such as an Associate's degree or certification, rather than a B.A. When the planet emerges from the 3rd house, it opposes the Midheaven, beginning a new career phase where those studies bear fruit. Since the planet then moves into the 4th house, the new endeavor may enable the person to work out of the home.

Check to see if the four angles form right angles to one another at birth, as often happens with the mutable cross, and in early degrees of cardinal signs. (For instance, the Ascendant may be around 4 degrees Libra, the IC around 4 degrees Capricorn, the Descendant around 4 Aries, and the Midheaven around 4 Cancer.) If this is so, a planet transiting one angle aspects all four over a couple of years. In these four-dimensional epochs, the very foundations of a person's life can be transformed. Career, committed relationships, appearance, and living situation are vastly different from the onset.

The Millennial Challenge—
Getting Past the Personal to the Universal

My teacher, Richard Idemon, made a distinction between personal, social, and universal signs—a fruitful division. He felt that the first four signs—Aries to Cancer—are most focused on personal development. The second four—Leo to Scorpio—are intensely concerned with relationships. The final four—Sagittarius to Pisces—are most oriented toward collective concerns. This is a generality, because we all know Cancers who stay up nights worrying about the ozone layer and Aquarians who ask, "What's in it for me?"

Still, Pluto's entry into Sagittarius ushered in an era when Uranus, Neptune, and Pluto are all in the universal signs. This will remain the case until most of us have gone on, leaving our grandchildren to reap what we have sown. These placements require that we look beyond ourselves for a more global perspective. We are increasingly asked to put aside personal concerns for the good of the collective. It is hard to know whether humanity will evolve in that direction fast enough, but we are all being challenged to try.

CHAPTER TEN

How Aspect Analysis Illuminates Chart Comparison

W e've covered plenty of ground in this book, but there is always much more to learn—one reason why astrology never loses its fascination. We've concentrated a great deal on aspects, as they are the basic building blocks of chart interpretation. To demonstrate that you can use these tools in situations beyond an individual chart, we'll do a bit of work here on chart comparison. The topic is one that can—and does—lend itself to whole tomes, but you'll get a taste of the process here, building on what we've already learned.

Preparing for a Relationship Reading

A relationship reading involves far more than the contacts between the two charts. It requires a thorough understanding of the planets in each individual chart. First, do a natal analysis of both charts. Look for planets in the Gauquelin sectors, for keynote planets, major configurations, and house and sign emphasis. When a keynote planet in one chart makes important contacts to the second chart, the dynamics and uses of that keynote planet will play an important part in the relationship. Furthermore, the relationship may also play an important part in the future development of that keynote's expression in the person's life.

Next, look at each birth chart to get a thorough understanding of what each expects and looks for when it comes to love. We tend to get into repetitive patterns in relationships, based not so much on the dynamics of the other person's chart as on our own. Because we tend to keep attracting and being attractive to the same type of individual, even when the externals appear different, our relationships keep working out the same way, until we work through our barriers. In each chart, look at the condition of Venus and Mars, and the 5th, 7th, and 8th houses, including any planets in those houses and the condition and placement of their rulers.

VENUS and its sign and aspects describe tastes and patterns in loving—how we show love, and how we, in return, hope to have love shown to us. Difficult aspects can show barriers to expressing love or to feeling love-worthy, thus there may be problematic choices in love and some history of heartbreak to overcome in order to be open to a new relationship.

MARS shows the active, go-get-'em drive to win over the other person, as well as the use of sexual energies. Without a Mars contact, the chase may never get underway. It also suggests how the person will handle the conflicts that inevitably arise with intimate ties.

THE 5TH HOUSE describes romance and how important it is to the person. One who is strong in the 5th and 8th houses, but weak in the 7th, may be more interested in romance than in commitment. If it comes to marriage, both partners must be willing to work at keeping the romance alive. In the charts of people of childbearing age, the 5th house may also describe children and how important they are to the person. If marriage is contemplated, it may be crucial to check for differences between the charts in this respect. If children are important and desirable to one but unwelcome to the other, this could present a serious conflict.

THE 7TH HOUSE (and/or Libra), when very strong, makes partnership and commitment very important. The subjects may not feel fulfilled in life without it. If the 7th house is very different from the 5th, this signifies that the person has different rules for commitment than for dating. Therefore, behavior may suddenly shift when marriage becomes an issue, much to the bewilderment of the partner. If a chart emphasizes the 5th and not the 7th, the person is hooked on the glow of courtship but may shun commitment.

THE 8TH HOUSE shows sexual tastes and patterns and how important sex is to each. Again, any major differences between the two 8th houses can cause a problem. Suppose that the man has a loaded 8th house, while the woman's 8th has only Saturn in Virgo. He is likely to be frustrated by her lack of interest in sex and, at some point, seek other outlets. Differences here can also pinpoint disagreements about the management of money and other joint resources—a major cause of marital conflict.

The House Configurations of Each Chart

Use a double-wheel chart blank, with two rings or layers instead of one. You will need two versions, the first with person A's planets in the inner wheel and person B's planets in the outer wheel, using person A's house cusps. The second version will show the reverse—person B in the inner ring and person A in the outer one.

It is instructive to see which houses in A's chart are filled with the planets of person B, and vice versa. For instance, if a number of the potential partner's planets fall in the client's 12th house, this suggests something about the relationship, whereas an activation of the 2nd house or the 7th house may show something entirely different. Sometimes, one of the attractions in a relationship is that the person fills out an empty house—that is, makes up for an area in which we are lacking. On the other hand, if a particular house is already full—with a stellium, for instance—and the other person's planets cluster there as well, it can make for an overemphasis on the concerns of that house. The relationship may be obsessive and lack balance.

Next, look for connections between the chart angles. Any planet in one chart that falls on an angle in the other is likely to be of major importance to the person whose angle is activated. If someone's Sun, Moon, or Venus falls on your Ascendant or Descendant, you can't help but notice them and are apt to be strongly drawn to them. On the other hand, if their Saturn or Pluto falls on one of those positions, you are likely to perceive them as a "heavy" and, most likely, want to avoid them. If the angle activated is the Midheaven, this individual may well play a role in your career or life path—sometimes spurring you on, sometimes holding you back, depending on the planet involved. When the IC is activated, the person makes you think of home—for better or worse—and may bring out patterns from your family of origin, or may spur your nesting instincts.

Conjunctions—The Juice in Chart Comparison

The real juice in a relationship comes from the conjunctions. The head-on collisions between your planets and the Other's are the things that make a relationship compelling—heaven or hell. The interesting thing is how often people reverse roles—that is, in a Mars-Saturn conjunction, the Saturn person may suddenly start to act Martian and the Mars person may begin to act Saturnine. Given a 3–5 degree orb, circle conjunctions between the two charts with a bright color. Sometimes I circle the more positive or easy conjunctions in the same turquoise pen I use for easy aspects in the birth chart, while circling the more difficult ones in pink. Again, the more visual clues you give yourself, the easier the big picture will be to grasp.

To illustrate the impact of conjunctions, do some concept lists for Venus-Mars conjunctions. This is an important contact in romance, for it heightens desire (Mars), attraction, and receptivity (Venus). To risk being archetypal (there I said it!), imagine a man with Mars in Aries and a potential partner with Venus in Aries. Now, many with these placements, especially with other planets in the picture, have learned to sublimate that passionate Aries nature, but others, especially those under 30, have not. Whether spoken or not, here is the dialogue you might imagine:

Mars in Aries	*Venus in Aries*
You're my kind of woman!	*You're my kind of man!*
Don't you dig my muscles?	*I love a good bod.*
Why wait? You know	*Why wait? You know*
you want me!	*you want me!*
I've got an hour now.	*I can live with that.*

Okay, okay, I'm exaggerating for effect. I know you're not like that, but you get the picture of the immediacy and compelling nature of the conjunction. Suppose instead that one person has Mars in Pisces and the other has Venus in Pisces. Recall chapter three, where we looked at the positive and the negative expressions of those placements. While both can be used in very evolved, spiritual ways in humanitarian or creative pursuits, when it comes to love and lust, it's easier for the unevolved expressions to creep in:

Mars in Pisces	*Venus in Pisces*
You're the woman of my dreams.	*You're the man of my dreams.*
I think about you all the time.	*I think about you all the time.*
Break out the champagne!	*Light the candles!*
Women have hurt me so much.	*Men have hurt me so much.*
I would never hurt you.	*I would never hurt you.*
My ex-wife still needs me.	*I have to visit my ex-husband in jail.*
You're not the woman I thought.	*You're not the man I thought.*
I'll never forget you.	*I'll never forget you.*

There's a distinct aroma in this combination of country music, line dancing, and booze. I could certainly be wrong—these could be two poets or two spiritual devotees who have finally found their soulmates after a lifetime of searching. My money is on the booze. Still, you'd want to see how each planet is configured in the birth chart and to interview the person as to how the planet is being used. Suppose it's the chart keynote—Venus in Pisces in the 9th, as part of a Grand Trine in water with Neptune and Jupiter. The chances of Venus being used spiritually are enhanced. Still, in this contact, you can't leave Mars out of the picture—and the gonads tend not to be terribly highly evolved.

The House Placement of a Conjunction

Remember that we are dealing with two people's wheels, so the house position of the conjunction in each person's chart is telling. Where the house placements are different (highly likely, unless the Ascendants and house cusps are close), each will experience the conjunction differently, depending on the house involved.

Suppose that one partner has the Venus-Mars contact in the 12th house, which is similar to Pisces or Neptune in some respects. Until the lesson is learned, a 12th-house Venus or Mars in the natal chart inclines one to secret affairs, the sort not readily acknowledged in public and often painful or self-defeating. To have the other's planet conjunct a 12th-house placement makes the affair nearly irresistible, yet very much a triggering of the old pattern. The result could be a clandestine affair that is highly romantic and compelling, yet ultimately painful.

In the other chart, the conjunction will most likely fall into a different house, and that placement tells something about what the relationship represents for that person. In the 8th house, the sexual dimension is reinforced. In the 4th, the person is more disposed to see this as someone with whom they can live comfortably—or it may evoke some of the patterns of growing up. In the 11th house, the Other is seen essentially as a pal—though with some spectacular perks to the friendship.

Because we've been considering a Venus-Mars conjunction, the love and lust dimension has been highlighted, but a relationship has many other facets. Look for Mercury contacts to see how good the communication and idea exchange would be. Are these two like-minded people? Contacts to the Moon show who nurtures who and how. Saturn contacts show the barriers and limitations, but also the capacity to commit and take on responsibility.

Depending on the nature of the relationship, other planetary pairs will step forward as crucial considerations—Moon and 4th-house contacts in family ties; Mars, Saturn, and Mercury in business connections; Jupiter and Mercury in teacher-pupil duos. Again, it is important to have a thorough sense of how each planet plays out in the individual chart before a complete picture of any given aspect in the chart comparison emerges.

Other Aspects in Chart Comparison

Next, plot the aspects between chart A and chart B. The process of finding these aspects is no different from finding them in the natal or transiting chart, although the orbs tend to be somewhat tighter—no more than 5 degrees for conjunctions or oppositions and 3 for squares or trines. (A quincunx may be of some importance, if no more than a couple of degrees apart, but sextiles are of negligible impact.) The task of finding aspects is simplified, because you aligned the two charts by sign and house when you put one person's chart in the other's wheel.

So that the page doesn't become so cluttered as to be unreadable, don't draw in the other aspects between the charts. Instead, list other chart contacts (major aspects only) on a separate piece of paper in columns like this:

Person A's Planets   *Aspect*   *Person B's Planets*   *Orb*

Rather than a conjunction between Mars and Venus in the two charts, let's see what happens with a square. What sort of dialogue (inner or outer) might you hear between Mars in Aries and Venus in Capricorn?

Mars in Aries	**Venus in Capricorn**
You're my kind of woman!	*You're hot, but not what I had in mind.*
When I see what I want, I go for it.	*Love takes time to develop.*
Let me peek at your undies.	*Let me peek at your resume.*
Why wait? You know you want me!	*I have responsibilities—a career to consider.*

The frustration, the challenge, as Venus in Capricorn plays hard-to-get, can actually spur Mars in Aries on. Thus, the square can be nearly as compelling as the conjunction, yet less prone to mutual satisfaction, since their natures and drives are at cross-purposes. Similarly, Mars in Gemini can be intrigued and stimulated by Venus in Pisces' elusiveness. The square between Mars and Venus still produces sizzling chemistry, but the rewards of the contact are intermittent and sometimes hollow. The tension resumes quickly and builds again. It's a dance, and it works for some. Hopefully, there are other major aspects, especially conjunctions, to make the relationship more than just passion. Shared values and interests, as evidenced in similarities between the two charts, make it easier to persist through the less compatible placements.

As you plot the aspects between the two horoscopes, look especially for planets in the partner's chart that might complete or activate a major configuration like a T-square or Grand Trine. When that happens, the relationship takes on some of the dynamics of that configuration. Suppose you have Jupiter in Leo trine Mars in Sagittarius, and the person you are interested in has Venus in Aries. You may well feel that you never have quite as much fun and enthusiasm as you do when that person is around. He or she lights your fire, giving you a kind of élan and *joi de vivre* you seldom experience on your own.

On the other hand, suppose you already struggle with a T-square of Mars, Saturn, and Mercury, and the other's Pluto sits on Mars or makes a T-square into a Grand Cross. They're in it with you, whatever the struggle might be, but it's hard to get out of the heaviness when they are around. Again, don't consider single contacts, but rather what each of the planets involved represents in the total picture.

And Now You're on Your Own!

Chart comparison is full of intricacies and checks and balances, and we can't hope to cover it adequately in this short exposition. What I really wanted to do here is to give you a starting place, drawing on tools you've already developed by following the process in this book. Aspects are the basic building blocks of astrology, and once you have a sense of how to take them apart and analyze them, you can use them in nearly every branch of astrology. You can now take a stab at electional, horary, or mundane astrology, progressions, lunar or solar returns, or any number of techniques. Granted, each such specialty has a body of particular knowledge accumulated over the centuries, but you have a foundation, at least. It is my hope that this book has empowered and emboldened you to do more and more chart interpretation on your own. Enjoy!

Bibliography

Angelou, Maya. *I Know Why the Caged Bird Sings.* New York: Bantam, 1984.

AstroComputing Services. *The American Atlas*, second edition, compiled by Thomas Shanks. San Diego: Astro-Computing Services, 1981.

Bergen, Candice. *Knock Wood.* New York: Simon & Schuster, 1984.

Cunningham, Donna. *Astrology and Spiritual Development.* San Rafael, CA: Cassandra, 1989.

———. *Astrology and Vibrational Healing.* San Rafael, CA: Cassandra, 1988

———. *Healing Pluto Problems.* York Beach, ME: Samuel Weiser, 1986.

———. *The Moon in Your Life.* York Beach, ME: Samuel Weiser, 1996.

———. *Moon Signs.* New York: Ballantine, 1988.

Dobyns, Zipporah. *Expanding Astrology's Universe.* San Diego: AstroComputing Services, 1985.

Gauquelin, Michel and Françoise. *The Gauquelin Book of American Charts.* San Diego: AstroComputing Services, 1982.

Idemon, Richard. *The Magic Thread: Astrological Chart Interpretation Using Depth Psychology.* Gina Ceaglio, ed. York Beach, ME: Samuel Weiser, 1996.

Lewis, Jim, and Ariel Guttman. *Astro*Carto*Graphy Book of Maps.* St. Paul, MN: Llewellyn, 1989.

Rodden, Lois. *ASTRO-DATA II.* San Diego: AstroComputing Service, 1980.

———. *ASTRO-DATA III.* Tempe, AZ: American Federation of Astrologers, 1986.

———, ed. *DataNews*, issues #29-75. Yucaipa, CA: 1984-1999.

Roseanne (formerly Barr). *My Life as a Woman.* New York: HarperCollins, 1989.

Sheehy, Gail. *Passages.* New York: Bantam, 1984.

Index

Angelou, Maya, 86, 130, 131, 165, 166
angles, 181
Aquarius, 154
   Ascendant, 34
   Sun, 35
Aries
   Ascendant, 42
   Sun, 35
Ascendant, 10, 23, 24, 25, 33, 181
   as a health point, 42
   last few degrees of a sign, 2
   Moon, 49
   outer planets transit to, 41
   Pluto near, 27
   Saturn near, 27
   Sun verses, 26
   Uranus, 49
aspects, 14, 15, 16, 81
   analysis, 185
   drawing them in, 17, 160, 161
   generational, 113
   hard, 81, 84
   having emphasis, 20
   Mercury-Saturn, 130
   missing, 20
   modify the Sun, Moon, Ascendant, 40
   soft, 103
   stressful and supportive, 18
Astrodrama, 37
Atro*Carto*Graphy, 9
authority figures, 85
Bergen, Candice, 38, 39, 66
Big Three, 40
birth data, 3
   source, 2
birth and death, 57
birth time, 1
Browning, Kurt, 110, 111, 115
Burnett, Carol, 38
Cancer
   Moon, 34
   qualities, 123
Cancer-Capricorn compatibility, 95
Capricorn
   Ascendant, 42, 34, 36, 38
   Moon, 36
   Sun, 36
chart comparison, 185, 188, 192
   conjunctions, 188
   house placements of

conjunctions, 191
T-square between the charts,
193, 194
charts, relocation, 9
Chronic Fatigue Syndrome, 42
clusters, 133
concept list, 82, 90
conflict, 92
conjunctions, 88, 188
transiting, 142
Dalai Lama, 121, 122
Daylight Savings Time, 2, 3
Descendant, 10, 27, 181
Dixon, Jeane, 5, 6, 7, 8, 12, 13, 14,
17, 18, 19, 20
Dobyn, Dr. Zipporah, 48, 66
Einstein, Albert, 86, 87
element, 48, 104
Sun, Moon, Ascendant in
same, 38
equal house system, 10, 14
Eye of God, 18, 154
Fabio, 77, 78
facilitators, 108
father, 24
Finger of Fate, 18, 126
forgiveness, 169
Gauquelin, Françoise and Michel, 8
Gauquelin sectors, 8, 37, 65, 67, 77,
79, 112, 130, 185
moving, 9
Gemini, 48
generational aspect, 113
Grand Cross, 194
Grand Trines, 114, 116, 119, 120,
193
Hawn, Goldie, 70, 71
Hepburn, Katherine, 38
hero, 159
horoscope
most influential factors, 23
preparing to read aspects and

transits, 160
House-Cusp controversy, 10
house meanings
3rd house, 13, 183
4th house, 191
5th house, 186
5th–10th house quincunx, 101
6th house Moon, 61
6th–9th house conflict, 94
6th–9th house sextile, 110
7th house, 13, 187
7th–10th house conflict, 94
8th house, 12, 187
8th–11th house conflict, 94
9th house, 12, 182
10th house, 48
11th house, 191
12th house, 182, 191
12th–7th house quincunx, 102
empty and active houses, 132
houses involved in opposition, 96
marriage, 13
Mercury opposite Saturn in
2nd and 8th, 99
Mercury and 3rd, 83
Mercury-Saturn in 2nd, 89
Mercury-Saturn in 5th, 89
Mercury-Saturn in 6th, 89
modifying key planets, 76
placement of planets in, 105
planet in 1st, 49
planet in 6th, 77
planet in 9th, 77
placement of planets in, 105
oppositions, 99
Saturn in 3rd, 85
Venus in Virgo in 5th, 63
house placements, 105
house position, 152
houses
empty, 11, 12, 13, 20
full, 11

modify planets, 76
stellium, 12
Sun in, 12
transiting Venus in 4th or
   10th, 146
transiting Venus in 5th or 8th,
   146
transiting Venus in 6th, 146
transiting Venus in 7th, 146
IC, 10, 181
Idemon, Richard, 97, 183
identity, 24
   crises, 43
infidelity, 146
introverts, 170
Jones, James Earl, 86
Jovial type, 73
Jupiter
   in Capricorn, 56
   functions of, 123
   in Pisces, 76
   in Scorpio, 54, 55, 76, 123, 124
   signature, 76
   in Taurus, 76
   transit, 138
   in Virgo, 128
Jupiter-Saturn trine, 124
Koch system, 10
Lawlor, Gretchen, 160
Leo, 48
Lewis, Jim, 9
Libra
   Ascendant, 41
   Moon, 34
lunar thresholds, 44, 45
Lunar type, 72
major configurations, 119
major themes, 20
marriage compatibility, 95
Mars, 47, 186
   in Aries, 189, 193
   is 11th, 76

   in Gemini, 58, 59, 193
   in Pisces, 58, 59, 190
Martial type, 73
Matlin, Marlee, 85
mental in focus, 82
mentor, 130
Mercurial type, 73
Mercury, 47, 51, 82, 83
   in Aquarius, 91, 106
   and Aquarius blended, 52
   in Aries, 110
   in Aries opposite Saturn in
     Libra, 98
   in Aries sextile Saturn in
     Aquarius, 110
   in Cancer sextile Saturn in
     Virgo, 109
   in Capricorn sextile Saturn in
     Scorpio, 110
   in 5th, 76
   in Gemini square Saturn in
     Sagittarius, 98
   in Pisces, 106, 107
   retrograde, 168
   in Scorpio 51
   square Saturn, 86
   in Taurus opposite Saturn
     in Scorpio, 99
   in Taurus square Saturn
     in Scorpio, 97
Mercury-Saturn
   aspects, 88, 84, 93, 130
   conjunction, 86, 88, 89
   oppositions, 97
   sextiles, 114
   square, 92
   trines, 105
metaphysically challenged, 177
Michelsen, Neil, 2
Midheaven, 10, 181
miscommunication, 92
mode, 48

monogamy, 146
Moon, 23, 31, 32, 47
    Ascendant, 32
    in Cancer, 35, 37, 128
    in Scorpio, 51, 61
    Uranus aspecting, 45
natal planet
    difficulty of, 162
    unaspected or under-aspected,
        162
Nelson, Willie, 126, 127, 129
Neptune, 80, 179
    in Aquarius, 148, 150
    influence of, 149
    in Scorpio, 113
    transiting, 149
Neptune-Uranus conjunction in
        Capricorn, 162
Neptunian type, 74
"on the other hand", 98
Onassis, Jackie, 89
opposite
    houses, 99
    signs, 99
oppositions, 94, 95, 96, 97
    Mercury-Saturn, 97
orb, 16
Other, 97, 129, 147
    dealing with the, 96
outer-planet people, 75
oyster and the pearl, 83
O'Donnell, Rosie, 155, 157
personal signs, 183
personality
    ascendant, 31, 32
    behavior, 23
    Cancer Moon and dependency,
        33
    changes with outer-planet
        transits, 180
    dysfunctional families, 24
    ego and the Sun, 173

father, 35
full functional families, 25
growth catalysts, 170
hard aspects to Sun, Moon,
    Ascendant, 40
inner and outer Mom, 169
Jupiter functions, 55, 56
long-standing issues, 162
major transits to Sun or
    Moon, 161
maturation through transits, 159
Moon functions, 44
Moon in Capricorn, 32
Moon-Saturn aspect, 32
mother, 35
motivation, 23
natal Sun-Saturn aspect, 174
Pluto, 53
relationships, 186
strong Taurus emphasis, 49
Sun, 31, 32
Taurus reaction to transits, 173
12th-house Sun, 27
Venus, Libra, Taurus, 49
Pisces
    Ascendant, 34
    Moon, 35
    qualities, 123
Placidus system, 10
planet
    angular, 37
    keynote, 185, 186
    stationary, 86
planetary
    functions, 52
    pair, 82
    signatures, 8
    types, 80
    planets affected by signs, 50
    on the angles, 8
    become keynotes, 65
    in houses, 61

modified by signs and houses, 76
retrograde, 160
Pluto
angles to the Moon, 169
crosses the Ascendant, 182
functions, 53
into Sagittarius, 143, 154, 183
was in Scorpio, 154
transits, 162
Plutonian type, 75
Pottenger, Mark, 2
power, unconscious fears about, 182
progressions, 158
psychological profile, developing a, 84
quincunx, 100, 126, 128
placements in Virgo, 154
reading the chart
Neptune, 179
visual survey, 4–5
reading the horoscope
dual wheel charts for companions, 187
panic states, 168
patterns, 175
planetary modifiers, 76
Pluto at midlife, 176
question in history of previous transits, 178
relationships, 185
significant transits, 161, 162
spotting critical zones, 165
transiting conjunction, 142
transiting inconjunct, 153
transiting opposition, 147
transiting sextiles, 152
transiting squares, 145
transiting trines, 150
transits only set off the birth chart, 177
Uranus aspects to all four angles, 168

Reagan, Ronald, 9
relationship
reading, 185
signs, 183
relationships, 186
planets and houses, 186
Your Mars to the Other's Saturn, 189
Your Venus to the Other's Mars, 189
retrograding, 160
Roseanne, 29, 30, 66
Rule of Three, 177
Sagittarius
Mercury-Saturn conjunction, 89
Saturn, 82, 83, 143
in Aquarius, 110, 128
in Cancer square Mercury in Aries, 93
in cardinal signs, 98
conjunct the Moon, 76
functions of, 123
in Gemini, 106
and maturity, 90
in Pisces, 123, 124
in Scorpio, 106, 107
in Scorpio square Mercury in Aquarius, 93
over the Sun, 173
in Taurus, 91
transits, 139, 143
in Virgo square Mercury in Sagittarius, 92
Saturnine type, 74
Scorpio
Mercury-Saturn conjunction, 89
qualities, 123
self-esteem, 24
self-worth, 36
sextiles, 104, 108
Shanks, Thomas, 2
Sheehy, Gail, 174

signs, dismantling of, 48
  Pisces and Gemini differences, 58
soft aspects, 103
Solar type, 72
Squares, 92, 94
stationary periods, 140
subpersonalities, 133
Sun, 23
  and ascendant, 27
  in Cancer, 101, 123, 124
  conjunct Pluto, 76
  functions of, 24, 123
  and Moon, pairing, 34
Sun-Ascendant clash, 29
Sun-Jupiter trine, 124
Sun, Moon and Ascendant, combining, 35
Sun-Moon aspects, 34
Sun-Saturn trine, 124
T-square, 133, 180, 193, 194
Taurus, 48
  Ascendant, 34
transiting
  when aspect is repeated, 162
  inconjunct, 153
  opposition, 147
  Pluto, 145
  sextiles, 152
  square, 145
  trines, 150
  Uranus in Aquarius, 153
  Uranus' patterns, 151
transits, 41, 137
  ASC/DSC, 161
  Chicken Little syndrome, 168
  difficult, 177
  facing difficult potentials of, 176
  hard and soft angles, 162
  hitting all the angles, 183
  important, 138, 160

introverts view, 170
Jupiter, 138
  to keynote planets, 162
  life-transforming angles, 181
  to MC/IC, 161
  to major configuration, 161
  men and Moon, 44
  Moon, 44
  to natal aspects, 137
Neptune, 179
Neptune to Ascendant, 42
Neptune-sensitized person, 180
outer-planet, 140
overview of, 159
Pluto, 162, 172
Pluto square Venus, 145
Pluto to Sun, 43
Pluto transiting Venus, 144
retrograde, 160
Saturn, 139, 143, 178
Saturn in Aries, 41
Saturn at different ages, 174
Saturn-Moon, 170
Saturn over Sun, 173
Saturn-sensitized person, 180
a series of, 171
stationary periods, 140
strongly Plutonian reactions to Pluto, 180
Sun, 43, 173
from 10th to 4th, 148
timing of, 139
women and the Sun, 44
trines, 104
  elements and, 104
  Mercury-Saturn, 105
universal signs, 183
Uranian type, 74
Uranus, 80
  in Aquarius, 101, 151
  aspects the MC, 181

and Neptune in
    Capricorn, 154
Uranus in Virgo, 113
    sextile Neptune in Scorpio, 113
Venus, 63, 143, 186
    in Aries, 153, 189
    in Capricorn, 76, 193
    Functions, 175
    in Gemini, 60, 61, 150, 151, 152
    in Leo, 148, 149, 150
    in Pisces, 60, 63, 175, 190, 193
    in Sagittarius, 144
    in Scorpio, 50

    in Taurus, 113
    in Virgo, 145, 147
Venus-Neptune conjunction, 179
Venusian type, 73
Virgo
    Ascendants, 36
    Mercury-Saturn conjunction, 89
    Moons, 36
    quincunx placements in, 154
    Sun, 35
    visual overview, 21
Yod, 18, 126, 128, 133

Donna Cunningham received a Master's degree in social work from Columbia University. In 1969 she began her astrological practice and subsequently received professional certification by Professional Astrologers, Inc. and the American Federation of Astrologers. With over 30 years of counseling experience as a certified psychotherapist, she uses various healing tools—such as flower essences, guided meditation, and visualizations—in her astrological work. She has been speaking at national and international astrological conferences since 1970 and has written hundreds of articles. She is the author of *An Astrological Guide to Self-Awareness*, *Healing Pluto Problems*, and *The Consulting Astrologer's Guidebook*. She is also the advice columnist for *Horoscope*. Donna currently lives in Portland, Oregon.